To Joan

May your birthday
be full of joy.
always

Much love,
Dee

It's Time

It's Time

Narratives on Illness, Aging, and Death

Dolores L. Christie

CASCADE *Books* · Eugene, Oregon

IT'S TIME
Narratives on Illness, Aging, and Death

Cascade Books
An Imprint of Wipf and Stock Publishers
199 W. 8th Ave., Suite 3
Eugene, OR 97401

www.wipfandstock.com

PAPERBACK ISBN: 978-1-5326-8079-3
HARDCOVER ISBN: 978-1-5326-8080-9
EBOOK ISBN: 978-1-5326-8081-6

Cataloguing-in-Publication data:

Name: Christie, Dolores L., author.

Title: It's time : narratives on illness, aging, and death / Dolores L. Christie.

Description: Eugene, OR: Cascade Books, 2019

Identifiers: ISBN 978-1-5326-8079-3 (paperback) | ISBN 978-1-5326-8080-9 (hardcover) | ISBN 978-1-5326-8081-6 (ebook)

Subjects: LCSH: Older people—conduct of life. | Aging—Religious aspects—Christianity. | Death—Religious aspects—Christianity.

Classification: HQ1061 .C4575 2019 (print) | CALL NUMBER (ebook)

Manufactured in the U.S.A.   NOVEMBER 8, 2019

"This Is My Body" first appeared in *Emmanuel, The Magazine of Eucharistic Spirituality.* Reprinted with permission.

"A Trip to the CABG Patch" originally appeared as "Rerouted," in *Commonweal* ©2014 Commonweal Foundation. Reprinted with permission. For more information, visit www.commonwealmagazine.org.

Scripture texts in this work are taken from the New American Bible, revised edition© 2010, 1991, 1986, 1970 Confraternity of Christian Doctrine, Washington, D.C. and are used by permission of the copyright owner. All Rights Reserved.

"Life's friends grow together like forest things,
twined together more with time.
Yet when they die, those ties still bind."

Table of Contents

Acknowledgments

COOKS NEED FARMERS, PICKERS, and producers before they can create wonderful meals. Artists require paints and canvas, actors require scripts, directors, make-up artists, and designers. In a beautiful quilt, pattern, pieces, and strands of thread must make a marriage.

So too, a written work has many "authors." My long-suffering husband, Dick, read each narrative, more than once. He encouraged me at every step, corrected and advised with careful eyes and critical comments. He tolerated take-out dinners and distracted time. Kathleen W. Fitzgerald and Dorothy Valerian read much of the almost-there product and offered suggestions. Robert Valerian and John Christie contributed prudent counsel. The decision-making schema was suggested to me over forty years ago by George Kanoti, PhD. Thanks to you all.

A special debt of gratitude is due to Jim Buettner, Nanci and John Volpe, and Karen Kozsey and family. Without their indulgent permissions and suggestions some of these narratives would not appear. I am grateful to many anonymous people, whose random words, unique stories, or deep feelings found their way into these pages.

I appreciate the help and soothing verbal Valium meted out generously by the support system at Wipf and Stock. An author, certainly a short one, rises on the shoulders of those who believe in her. She offers her work in their honor. I can do no less.

Introduction

Tell me a story
Tell me a story
And then I'll go to bed.

AS CHILDREN, WE DEVELOP a taste for story. From Snow White to *Star Wars*, from the biblical Garden of Eden to today's *Game of Thrones*, stories captivate our imagination. Like a mystery novel or a stellar movie, the pieces in this book can be engaged for their own sake, without any additional purpose.

But stories are insidious. They seed values, lessons, and emotionally packed paradigms that shape our moral identity. Fairy tales portray vulnerability conquered by hope or bravery—sometimes with a little help from little friends. Movies explore the potential for courage, love, the overcoming of evil. Without announcing it, good narratives do much more than entertain. They embed in us values and norms that remain, like recombinant DNA. They continue, as a Jesuit friend remarked, to "populate the heart."

These additions influence our actions. Everyone's personal moral compass retains stories drawn from unique experiences and from the specific social and cultural environment we inhabit. Like apps on a computer, they store the tools and information we access when we confront decisions. Although they are not always a conscious referent, stories tend to determine *and* limit how we think about and prioritize values. In turn, this data bank affects what we choose.

Some stories are difficult. Like children who cover their eyes when a movie gets scary, we keep buried in the closet of our fears things we do not wish to face. We experience illness, but with luck it rarely attracts our attention for more than a short course of cough syrup or a passing pimple. Serious illness is not something we wish to contract or even to consider. It happens to other people in other worlds.

We encounter aging, but for the most part we prefer its embodiment out of sight in forgotten storage places we call "homes." We see the elderly in television ads for miracle drugs. Their infirmities are "touched up" like doctored photos of aging celebrities. Only happy faces of the old are portrayed, full of smiles oozing of medicinally-enhanced youthful vigor. We prefer not to notice the softly spoken side effects whispered beneath those ads: "Deaths have happened."

In American culture *death* is tacitly a dirty word. We all know it, but we do not speak it in polite company. When we must, it gets sanitized into "passed on," "in a better place," "gone home." And then we squirm with discomfort and change the subject.

This book turns a bright, sometimes painful, light on serious life situations that in time invade everyone's life. Each piece poses practical and moral questions for patients, for families, for professionals that accompany those in distress. Some stories are likely to resonate with experiences we ourselves have had, dealt with, and tried to forget. Nevertheless they provide an opportunity to heal the past, think about future possibilities (perhaps the better word is *probabilities*), and how we might adjust to them. These are not the only stories that consider these issues, but they are the ones I know.

For professionals there is the opportunity to think about how patients and families exist, fleshed out beyond their allotted fifteen-minute visits. Poignant and relevant backstories cannot be captured fully by sanitized data on the electronic chart. For some professionals, it may assuage guilt for regretted decisions. ("My patient died. I should have done more. Now I understand that I did the best I could, under the circumstances."). The stories remind and reassure that none of us is unique or perfect in facing hard choices.

Although not its purpose, this can be called a selfish, even voyeuristic book. To a greater or lesser degree, all serious writing draws from the treasures and tears of the author's experience. For me, some of the narratives in this book reprise the gold of gratitude and joy from my own life. Others I retrieved reluctantly from protective personal vaults, locked places that hid the tarnish of sadness and grief.

Some of the stories draw from real situations. Like the scavenged scraps of some old bag lady, bits and pieces are saved, perhaps to be organized and retold. But true stories are much more than utilitarian detritus. Revealed here for the reader, they are infinitely precious shards of life from the experience of heroic people. They are like beautiful—perhaps broken—shells that once caught a sunglassed beach comber's eye and were tucked into a sandy pocket for later perusal, sometimes with sadness. For whatever reason, I have been afforded a privileged window into others' journeys. They left behind gifts of wisdom, of endurance, of acceptance, of struggles with difficult decisions, or one last futile battle.

Most of the stories are fiction. Yet even these are "true," in the sense that illness, aging, and death are universal experiences. They are embellished to make them richer, the "thick description" that ethicists favor.

Finally, this is a work product of a professional moral theologian, college professor, and clinical ethicist. It uses the salient salvage from forty years of cases discussed in undergraduate and graduate classes, in tense meetings with distraught families, or in hastily called conferences in institutional settings.

During my many years of teachings, classroom discussions illustrated vividly how each person brings personal experience to decision-making. In one memorable bioethics class, I posed a case about the efficacy of feeding tubes. Students reacted spontaneously with strong opinions. The traditional-age students thought such devices were a good intervention. "My uncle lived three happy years with artificial feeding." Returning students, many experienced nurses who had worked in nursing homes or intensive care units, testified strongly against their use. "I hated to see these demented people, tied to tubes and to lives left with no humanity." Each group brought its own story. We all learned. Often, when cases I used drew on own my personal experience, members of the class forced me to revisit decisions I had made in the past. They raised elements never considered in the urgency and emotional stress of real time, elements that might have produced a better choice.

The first part of this book considers illness. Persons in the best years of their lives are faced with serious, sometimes deadly diseases. They must choose how or even whether to undergo debilitating treatment, or even interventions that blot out months or years of their lives before they work sufficiently. Others deal with choices for their children or their parents. Older people face surgery or disruption of their lives, perhaps invading the lives of those they love and who love them. Spouses and friends must walk with or walk away from the painful journeys of others. Parents and offspring are forced to decide for others. When it's time, it's time.

The second part looks at the upside and downside of aging. A percentage of older people can age in place, some effectively. A ninety-year-old still plants annuals each year in her garden. Another volunteers for Meals-on-Wheels or hopes to clean her basement before debility or death force other plans. Others' circumstances place them in long-term care. Some fight the onslaught of time with denial. Aging brings complicated moral choices to spouses, care givers, and even knocks on the secured doors of tenured professors or hospital administrators.

The third group of stories takes on the serious reality of death. One faces this actuality passively, either with optimism, perhaps a soothing belief in afterlife, or with an assessment that the current life is no longer livable. Another opts for a quicker ending, eschewing natural death for quicker means. Someone else decides to take on the full-court press of every available treatment.

When the tales are told, I cannot deny that professional readers or reviewers will find moral issues lurking in every story. Some may want to explore these issues more deeply. Their scholarly selves will look for pitchy questions at the end of each essay. They will be disappointed.

As a professed professor of things morals, I apologize for my reluctance to distract from the stories themselves with the anticipated didactic addition after each chapter. Therefore, only after the narratives were completed did I put on my sober ethicist's hat. At the end of the book there is a surprise for disappointed readers: two appendices.

Appendix A lays out a simple schema for making moral decisions specific to the three topics of the book. It is intended as a referent for the questions that follow. It will be helpful particularly for those without a background in systematic moral thinking, perhaps even beyond the scope of this book.

Appendix B offers questions tailored to each episode in the book. These highlight moral aspects of each essay, sometimes exploring its more emotional and concrete dimensions. They are intended to facilitate group discussion.

It is the hope, of course, that some readers will engage the stories for their own sake, to appreciate that moral issues cross both the age and gender spectrum, that some things are painful and complicated. They should feel free to skip the Appendices. Others will find in-depth reflection valuable in their professional careers. Busy doctors will understand better the anxiety and concerns of patients. Today's medical system seems to accord hegemony only to technology and the cost-efficient fifteen-minute visit: the alcoholic liver in the hospital room at the end of the hall rather than Mrs. Jones, the mother of five dissolved in tears. Professionals in training might learn something that will allow them to see their patients more as people with value and values, rather than medical problems to be solved.

Finally, the book honors the sacred past of many. I offer my deepest respect and gratitude to those who are memorialized here. Likely it will be painful for some to read, cathartic or reassuring for others. Most of all I hope it will be instructive and troubling in a good way, one that will help anyone who reads it to grow in compassion, understanding of self and others, and better at making decisions.

The optimistic song from *Annie* reminds us: "The sun will come out tomorrow." It is playing on the radio as I write. It's time to remember that pain and loss do not last forever.

Illness

Impotence

"There is no cure for ALS; nor is there a proven therapy that
will prevent or reverse the course of the disorder."

(MEDICINENET.COM)

IN MY MIND I see the amber cylinder: precious Percocet perched on the
shelf in the medicine cabinet. It makes its home between my wife's small
plastic square of dental floss and the almost-empty tube of toothpaste.
There is probably enough pain killer in the bottle to shut down my liver
and end my life. Too bad I was unable to reach it. Even though the house is
wheelchair friendly, there are some places that wheels cannot breach.

Mary and I moved to that home in the country about three years ago.
It was just after I had been diagnosed. ALS—Lou Gehrig's disease—is not
something one wants to see on the medical chart, even one as thick as mine.
I saw the same family doctor for many years. He was near retirement at the
time of my diagnosis. He shepherded me through childhood rashes and a
rash jump off a ski slope in my teens. Reassuring and optimistic about my
recovery at the time, he referred me to an orthopedic specialist. He was
right! I was back on the slopes the following winter.

The day he delivered the damning news about Lou Gehrig's disease he
looked heavy-hearted and powerless. He named and explained the trajectory of the illness. I left his office that day alone in every way, carrying a
burden much heavier than my extensive medical chart. And this time the
doctor could not reduce the weight.

At first, I excused the stiff muscles as the result of a long and strenu-
ous day of baseball. My buddies and I saw ourselves still as teenagers: our

3

bodies invincible to the waves of age that seemed to hover on the horizon of low tide. We consumed a few beers through the afternoon and felt no fatigue, at least not until the next day. But this time a hot shower and a good night's sleep did not relieve the aches I felt. Nor did succeeding showers in the next few days.

Then there was the celebratory steak we had for our anniversary dinner several weeks later. I complained that it was a bit tough, hard to chew. Mary apologized and agreed, frowning as she swallowed a modest bite.

She kept telling me she had trouble understanding me when I spoke. "Yeah. Must be your hearing's going. Happens when you begin to age." I laughed. She did not. As wives do, she chided me when I appeared to drool. "Wipe your mouth!" I dutifully obeyed.

Summer came early that year. The house was getting too warm without the screens to usher in cooling evening breezes. The ritual of trading storms for screens was not one I particularly enjoyed. Nevertheless, it was time. Later I dismissed the persistent lethargy that followed the onerous process. It came, of course, from the hour I spent to pick up the mess from the storm window that shattered as I took it out. I must have grazed the door jamb. It dropped from my hands. Shiny shards exploded all over the front stoop. Between bending again and again to clean up, stretching to measure the space for a new window, *and* making two trips to the hardware store—the first measurement was not quite accurate—I had a right to be tired. This was not a job I counted on. Installing those screens and securing the storm windows in the basement left me tired and sweaty. And it was hot! Likely my sweaty hands caused me to drop it in the first place! Couldn't help it. Not my fault.

I began to notice a certain clumsiness that seemed to come more often. I'd pop a couple of pills to ease the grumbling muscles. Seemed to help. What I was feeling seemed unimportant. I wasn't even going to mention this stuff to the doctor at my yearly check-up that day, but I almost fell as I got up to leave his office. He frowned. "Ah, Doc, just missed a step. That's all."

The doctor suggested I sit back down and rest for a couple of minutes. He asked a few questions and checked some muscle strength to figure out what was going on. "Maybe we should run a couple of tests." The next time I saw him he confirmed the diagnosis. It wasn't simply a confluence of unrelated things like baseball and broken glass. It was ALS. The protective covers on my nerves were gradually disintegrating. The condition would progress until I was an invalid. And then I would die.

I Googled a lot that day, trying to find a reason or a remedy. Mary and I cried together, got angry at God and the universe, and finally sat down to decide what we should do. At the time we lived very close to a high-powered medical facility. We could see the emergency room from our second-floor bedroom. Some nights the sirens going to the ER woke us. They reminded us daily of what my serious illness might entail.

What would happen if I had an episode and got rushed to the hospital? Neither of us were particularly happy with the prospect of repeated hospital admissions. Not exactly your weekend splurge to Vegas! I am pretty doctor-averse. The only reason I kept my ritual of yearly check-ups was because of the long relationship with my doctor.

We agreed to sell the home where we lived happily for several years, even though we were sad to leave its convenient location and beautiful garden. We pictured a small one-floor cottage in the country, where the temptation to rush to medical care could be avoided. And there would be fewer windows! Mary was willing to go along with what I believed to be the best plan, given my dire prognosis.

If there were no cure, we might as well deal with reality. A single-story house in the woods was a perfect place to spend the limited measure of time together that we had left. And the clock was ticking. We bought a modest place, down sized, and got ready for the next step. Persistent questions about the disease were stored in tight mental boxes as we packed our belongings for the move. No point in dwelling on what we could not change. Hide it away and try to forget.

The new house was beautiful. It had three cozy bedrooms and a fireplace that yearned for a mid-winter blaze. Fallen branches from the mature maples in the yard offered ample kindling to stoke a fire. Mary collected them as they fell. We waited for winter and that warm fire.

Waking each morning, we listened to the birds' first song—a much better alarm clock than those sirens. We heard the last crickets as we fell into sleep each night. On days I felt strong enough, we walked hand in hand to the top of the hill near us to watch the sun go down. We knew the increments of time were slipping away. We wanted to squeeze every possible drop of good from them. I was still pretty functional, even driving.

Mary and I had talked about the progression of the disease. When the day came that I could no longer do these things, she was ready to pick up the slack. We married for better or worse. Let's cherish the better for now, before the predicted "worse" is all we had. Life was good. We almost forgot those dreaded letters: ALS. For now they were tucked away in one of those boxes from the old house, one that we planned never to open.

The first winter in the new house came and went gently. We watched the hoarded maple branches became ash as we cozied near the fire. Then came spring. It was warm and sunny one morning—a good day to buy the tomato plants for a bumper summer crop of salads in summer's promise. Mary stayed home, jealously guarding some time to herself.

I slipped awkwardly into the blue pickup, and turned on the radio. I loved to sing in the car, loud and unembarrassed. "Born in the USA. I'm a cool rocking daddy in the USA." Bruce Springsteen and I belted out the words. Life was good. ALS was on the back burner of my mind. I sang with abandon, one palm banging on the steering wheel in time with the music. "Born in the USA."

Thud! That awful sound that announces a collision. The truck hit me broadside as I entered the intersection. Neither of us saw the other because of the bend in the road and the thick bushes all around. They tell me that the other guy got by with only scrapes. Neither of us could have known. The cars were towed, telltale glass marked the spot. (I hate broken glass!) He got a bandage, the badge of a bad cut. I got a free ride. The ambulance took me to the nearest hospital, ironically the one visible from our old house. My injuries were serious.

When I finally woke up my whole body was numb. My first thought was, "Wow, I haven't felt this good in quite a while." Realization came: I was in traction. They had given me pain killers to ease my discomfort. Bones were broken and blood was lost. It was going to take a long time for me to get better.

And I did, but during that prolonged hospital stay my ALS got worse. As the tidal wave of injuries from the accident began to subside, the dread disease littered its effects on the entire beach of my body. I could no longer move my legs and my breathing became more and more difficult. They put me on a respirator.

No, no. This is not what I wanted! The progression of the ALS and now the breathing apparatus make it impossible to speak. How could I tell them? Clearly Mary was reluctant to own the decision to remove the respirator. How could she sign what would amount to my death warrant? What would they think of her? How could she know that I would rather die than live like this: a mute mess of my former self? My advanced directive—the doctor had suggested that I sign one early in the disease—said only that I did not want "extraordinary measures" taken, but the standard form added the words, "if I were near death." The Machiavellian machines of modern medicine keep that option just beyond my choice. This was exactly what prompted the move to the country. How could this be happening?

The hospital provides intubated patients with a kind of speak and spell thing. Such toys are advertised on television in compelling Christmas ads. Light-weight and rectangular, it is the kind of gift a small child would love to discover under the holiday tree. Its tiny alphabet, in brightly-colored letters, is accessible with a gentle push. Behind its sterile plastic face are pictures of smiling stick figures in hospital beds, one sitting up, one at a forty-five-degree angle, one lying flat. A single push tells the human care giver how the patient wishes to be positioned. If the care giver comes. There is a row of yellow faces, from very happy to very frowning and sad. A patient can indicate the face that describes the level of comfort or pain.

Ironically, I can no longer prompt my *own* face to elicit these emotions. Frowns and smiles are beyond my strength. Likewise, I can no longer fill my lungs to push out the frustrated scream that every fiber of my being feels. Baseball and Bruce Springteen are missing from my tool box of pleasurable activities. But still, with a pencil held between my teeth and great effort I can push those tiny alphabet buttons to communicate my wishes.

With concentration and an excruciating amount of time I press out words. The touch touches those around me. They understand. I tell Mary that I love her, even though I can only eke out the five letters that say, "Luv u M." These small crumbs of "conversation" sap my strength, leaving me exhausted. Mary tightens my hand, and her silence follows. Like her biblical namesake, she keeps all things in her heart. Oh, I so want to hold her again, to love her again with my body!

This has to end. Like the protective covers on my nerves, the layers of my life peel away. Because our insurance is bare bones—we cannot afford high-end policies—the bills mount. We put aside some money when we sold the larger house, but that buffer is almost gone. Mary tries to keep this from me, but I know. At least my brain still works!

One day I ask to have this end. It takes a long time to punch in the words. Mary cannot hide her feelings. Tears fill her eyes and overflow, as she tries to avoid the truth. We both know. More medical bills will not only devour our remaining savings but likely will cause her to lose our house.

I move the pencil once again. "Turn off." It takes me a long time to punch out the death sentence, but it's what I want. A resolute rainbow of letters spells out my wishes. No, that's not true. What I want is to be in my own home. To spend my shortened life in my own bed: no monitors or midnight noises to disturb my sleep. So much simpler. So much easier for Mary. The hospital offers another alternative. They speak of "sliding me over" to a full-time care facility. No, that's not what I want either.

At times I think of legendary Inuit grandmas who walked out onto ice floes, choosing death over starvation for their people held back by the slow step of the elderly. These women decided to become that one less person to feed, as the tribe, desperate for food, followed caribou across the frozen land. I am afraid, but also resolute. I, too, owe something to my wife, friends, care givers. This is not suicide. It is simply facing reality and turning off some machines. It's time.

Row 30

"Pain is temporary. Quitting lasts forever."

(LANCE ARMSTRONG AND SALLY JENKINS,
EVERY SECOND COUNTS)

THE CONNECTING FLIGHT FROM Houston was cancelled. Predictably, there were only a few seats left on the substitute. I looked at my new boarding pass. Ugh. My travel partner was much more fortunate than I: a seat half way up on the aisle. He had priority boarding. My seat was probably the worst in the plane: last row, in the middle. I guess it's the luck of the draw. Sometimes the gods are arbitrary when they make decisions for others. Some people are tall; some are short. Some are fertile; others not so much. Some are healthy; others . . . .

It was time. The plane began to board. We filed in slowly. I passed my friend, already settled in an exit row. I smiled weakly. Subdued and shoe-horned into the rear of the sardine-packed airplane is punishment usually reserved for those who book late or fly standby. I secured my seat belt and settled into the prospect of a long trip. I tried to be considerate, careful to keep my elbows tucked into my sides. There is little comfort in the middle seat.

It was late in the month; the in-flight magazine was missing pages. Someone had removed the game pages. Alas! No crossword puzzle to pass the time after the perky flight attendant served tepid tea and tired pretzels. In any case, my brain was tired from preparation for the trip. I rummaged for the paperback in my carry-on. That would have to do.

A seasoned flyer never chooses Row 30. The only saving grace is its location near the bathroom, a good or bad thing, depending on one's needs and sense of smell. First to enter; last to leave. Those trapped far back in the plane during disembarking can only stretch and gather "personal belongings," as they watch more fortunate passengers collect their random detritus and deplane.

After we got into the air, Miss Perky finally reached our row. "Would you like a snack?" "Sure." The refreshment—if you could call it that—did not take long to consume. Miniature napkin stuffed into a sad paper cup. Debris collected. Exciting part of trip over. Check.

Our meeting was on the west coast, so this flight was going to be a long one. After the first hour or so I tired of the novel. The characters were well defined, but the prose was mediocre. When will writers learn to avoid overdoing adjectives?

I tried to sleep, but rest is difficult in the middle row. The only place to rest one's head is behind. Yawn. A glance at the watch: one more hour before landing. Then I noticed my neighbor.

She was a young woman, thin, with bottled reddish-brown curls. Her hair was nicely styled, and slightly long. While dark rings shaded under her eyes suggested long-trip fatigue, her color was good. She was well-dressed, maybe in her early forties. No kids? No husband? Must be a professional woman, away on a business trip, tired from too many late nights and too many hours sitting in airports. She read a hardback novel, its plastic library cover betraying its origin. Hope her book was better than mine!

We struck up a conversation. "Where are you from? Ah, going home then. That's nice. I'm off to a convention. Long flight, not all that comfortable. Tell me about your family." Then I noticed the plastic wrist band on her left arm. This stylish woman was not traveling on business. She was returning home from half way across the country for cancer treatment, a recurring unpleasant life pause, one which she entered frequently. This odious medical intervention had extended her life for over a decade. The shadows under her eyes took on a darker meaning.

When she was barely thirty, the family doctor confirmed the nature of the telltale lump. She rarely went to a doctor in those days, but she noticed a tenderness in her breast. At first she did not pay much attention. Married with two young children, her life was consumed with other things. "It can't be important. I have lunches to pack, carpools to arrange, diapers to change." From time to time she checked the tiny knot. Probably related to breast feeding. After she weaned her baby, though, the lump was still there—and larger.

By the time she saw the doctor the hungry cells had already breached the lymph node barrier and begun to ravage her body. The doctor offered a dire prognosis. It was devastating and definitive: she was going to die. Treatments were available, but he was not optimistic about their efficacy. The literature indicated that they promised a little more time, but the side effects were not pleasant. It was unlikely that she would see her children grow up. She would never hold *their* children in her arms. Tears and shock mingled as she drove home that day.

Stunned, she and her husband talked about what to do. She was young. The children needed her. Her husband did, too. Maybe she would be the outlier. Studies are not perfect. She elected to begin treatment. Her primary care doctor recommended a specialist. Fortunately, her husband's company provided insurance choices.

The oncologist initiated a mild course of chemo that spared her the usual nausea and hair loss. "We'll make it work for you. We won't give up hope."

For a time the protocol seemed to be successful. She and her doctor laughed about her being the poster girl of hope. They should write an article! Then he developed a serious illness of his own and had to close his practice. She was devastated.

Desperate for something that might work, she turned to a national treatment cancer center. There was a well-respected hospital near her home, but they did not take her insurance. Sometimes American insurance companies are parsimonious in what they cover, particularly if your ability to pay is limited. Young and on a tight budget, she and her husband agreed earlier to an inexpensive company plan primarily to cover medical exigencies of the children. Who could predict such a life-limiting illness for such a young woman? And now she carried that onerous label. She had that "pre-existing condition" that the insurance choices offered by her husband's work did not cover in their "affordable" plans. Nevertheless, there must be some place she could go.

She searched for another treatment center, but there were none near the small town outside of San Diego where she lived. That was why she was on this plane, in Row 30. Her treatment required periodic travel halfway across the country. Not only was the treatment debilitating, but the long plane ride sapped what energy remained when she was done. Accessible and affordable life-sparing care for a life-taking illness was a must, if she wanted to live. What else could she do?

Even with treatment, the cancer would not be denied its territorial advance. Now its kingdom spread not only to lymph nodes but to major organs, including her liver and her spine. That was why she was seated today in the plane's last row. She could no longer accept the responsibility of a seat in the exit row, to which she had been assigned originally. My traveling companion had lucked out, at this woman's expense. Now the site of constant pain, her spine was not strong enough to allow her to open the emergency door.

Nevertheless, the aggressive interventions kept her alive for an amazingly long time. A practicing agnostic regarding miracle cures, I listened with interest. It was true. Amazingly she and her husband watched their children grow, marry, and have children of their own. The woman condemned to death years ago was now a grandmother! And she—against all odds—*was* able to hold those babies.

The flight attendant, now a bit less perky, came through to pick up discarded newspapers and other disposable items. Time to get rid of that outdated airline magazine! Dutifully we yielded our trash. We were reminded to check seat belts and prepare for landing. The temperature at our destination was moderate and rain was expected later in the day. We were coming into Gate B 45. "Thank you for flying with us today. Enjoy your day. Watch for shifting luggage in the overhead compartment."

The plane descended, hit the ground with only a minor hiccup, and moved along the runway. I saw my seat mate wince as we hit a bump. Almost immediately the cell phone in her purse rang. Her wan face exploded in a warm smile. Clearly eager to talk with the caller, she excused herself from our conversation and turned her attention to the phone. Her husband waited to pick her up. He confided that he remembered to bring scissors to cut off the plastic wrist band that identified her as "cancer patient." She certainly fit the latter part of that description: a *patient* woman of courage and optimism. She smiled in anticipation of seeing her family and being home. Surely this had not been a pleasure trip.

We taxied to the gate. After what seemed like hours the door to the cabin opened. A blast of cool air relieved the sweaty passengers near the door. It was time. Other phones rang, as passengers connected with their rides. We performed the rituals of readying to leave the plane. Standing in the aisle waiting for the other passengers to deplane; we exchanged good-byes, wished each other well and a long future.

The luck of the draw. Some people are born tall; others are short. Some are fertile; others not so much. Some are healthy; some are not.

I never saw this courageous woman again. So many people cross the paths of our lives for only an instant. We exchange pleasantries or profound stories. Just as the vast horizon viewed from an airplane is lost to view upon landing, short encounters preclude a view of the future.

I do not know what became of her. I expect she continued to battle that deadly disease, at least for a while. I hoped without reason that she might dance at the wedding of one of her grandchildren. We will not meet again to catch up on our respective lives. A chance encounter in Row 30: the final row in the airplane. It was comforting to know that it was not yet a metaphor for a final chapter in her life.

Red Sprinkles

"We know what we are, but know not what we may be."
(WILLIAM SHAKESPEARE)

I MET HER FOR the first time when announcements were over and we went to the lockers in the back of our newly-assigned freshmen homeroom. It was time to liberate our books for morning classes. She was not a graduate of my grade school, but her school was staffed by the same order of nuns that ran ours. She liked red and so did I. We hit it off right away. In fact, we became great buddies. Over those halcyon years we shared our dreams and giggled at our silly private jokes. Often when we double-dated, our escorts were left out of the conversation. Most of them never called again.

In freshman year she was a bit chubby, baby fat clinging to a grownup body. In college we called it the "freshman fifteen"; in high school we ignored it, mostly. We laughed about our mutual love of—some would say addiction to—the still-warm doughnuts available at a small shop on the way to the bus stop. Healthy dietary variety was the order of our day: red sprinkles on Monday, powdered sugar on Tuesday, etc. We liked Monday's best. But then things changed.

Mary Claire decided to lose some weight. In our junior year she elected to go on a diet, eschewing our daily treat. Instead of her usual lunch and mid-afternoon doughnuts she brought a polyploid grapefruit to lunch every day. Some of us bagged a sandwich from home or selected something from the cafeteria menu. Mrs. Sweeney's predictable pizza or soggy avocado-colored peas were available on the buffet next to the slinky jade jello and salty soup. The desserts were not quite as bad. They even offered

14

frozen custard with red sprinkles, but each day Mary Claire ate only that obese grapefruit she brought from home.

We all thought she was a bit strange. She did not consume it in the normal way, sliced in half and scooped out deliciously so the juice dripped from the serrated spoon. Rather it was attacked as if it were some over-grown orange: remove the peel and separate the sections. And after school we went directly to the bus stop. No more delightful doughnuts.

During the remainder of our high school years Mary Claire struggled on and off—literally—with her weight. She tried different diets, from the all protein (eat lots of hot dogs) to Weight Watchers (pay to monitor the drop off). She read everything she could find on nutrition and body image. Somehow the scale's message never pleased her. A bit like the Queen in the story of Snow White, she was never "the fairest of them all."

After we graduated and got accepted to colleges in different cities, we went our separate ways. Mary Claire got a scholarship to Stanford. I attended a small women's college in Columbus. Both of us were busy and, since she went to school on the west coast, we did not even get together on breaks. I lost touch with my dear friend. One year she scribbled a brief note on a Christmas card. She married a guy she met in college. They were living in San Jose, where he worked.

Mostly we both went on with our lives. Mine was invested in teaching first grade in Columbus, a year-by-year series of small children who never sat still and often called me "Mommy." I began graduate school. Life was complicated and demanding, but at least there was a doughnut shop near my school. Not as good as those wonderful cakes in Cleveland, but they did have some with red sprinkles. Eventually the kids exhausted me. Teaching small children is hard. It was time. I took my duds and dishes and returned home to Cleveland.

Several months after I was back, Mary Claire and I ran into each other quite by chance. Coincidentally it was on the street where that old bakery used to be. I almost didn't recognize her. She looked terrible. She was no longer even a bit overweight. In fact she was abnormally skinny. Her clothes fit her as they might a wire hanger. What happened to my friend?

She told me that she and her husband divorced. He found someone else. Since there were no children and she just needed to forget the whole sorry episode, she came back to Cleveland to live with her mom. Then Mom died, and now Mary Claire rattled around in her mom's old house.

She and her brother quarreled over who should get the property and were now estranged. He was rather well off and didn't need the house. Yet he felt entitled to it. Finally he relented, but things between them were never the same.

She was out of work and struggling. Her college degree in art had not produced a paying job here. She took in sewing to make ends meet, barely. When things got really tough, she had a few paintings of her own left. She sold them little by little. Partly because she was trying to be frugal (she said), she went back to her grapefruit diet. This time there were rarely two other meals to keep her going.

"It's hard to cook for yourself," she mused. "Besides, fasting is good for one's character. Don't you remember what the nuns taught us about the efficacy of suffering? I just offer it up for the poor souls. If God calls me soon, that's OK, too. Maybe better! What exactly do I have to live for anyway? When I sell the last painting and the money runs out, God will call me. I'll know that it's time."

I was devastated and felt guilty for not keeping in touch. We had been so close in high school, the yin and yang of an inseparable relationship. Whatever happened to Sam and Montgomery, the silly names we gave each other? It was our code, when we passed notes in class.

It was time to make amends. I suggested we get together. I wanted to tell her about the guy I was about to marry "in my old age," but it seemed inappropriate given the painful story she just told me. Would she consider a lunch? "No, let's just get a cup of tea, maybe sometime next week?"

We met at the local Starbucks. I was early. Before she arrived, I ordered my large black tea and a chocolate chip cookie (buy one, get one free) and staked out a seat. When she sat down with her tea ("Small, please"), she refused my second cookie. After catching up on other stuff, I told her about my wedding plans. Maybe she could be one of the bridesmaids. She seemed excited. We talked about the color of the dresses and the handmade lace veil—my mother's—that went so well with my gown. It was as if we never missed a step in our relationship.

When it was time to go, I reminded her, "Call me when you decide about being a bridesmaid. We'll have to set up a date for you to meet my Ray." I left the remainder of my neglected cookie. It seemed insensitive to eat the rest of it while Mary Claire consumed only her tepid tea. We hugged and parted. I could feel her shoulder bones, even under her heavy sweater.

Three weeks later, after she met the other attendants at the fitting for the dresses, the call came that something had come up and she could not attend the wedding. I picked it up on the machine. She didn't call my cell. Did it have something to do with the fact that food was central to the planned celebration? My mind went immediately to one word: anorexia.

The date for the wedding grew closer. While I was disappointed that she was not coming, I did not think much about Mary Claire. There were invitations and fittings, flowers to order, and friends almost forgotten to add to the guest list. Presents were coming and thank you notes were on the horizon.

Then one day the mailman brought a flimsily wrapped small box. I recognized the return address. It was a house I knew well. On lazy summer days Mary Claire and I had dreamed together in its backyard: "We will marry really cute guys, and your oldest son will marry my beautiful daughter. Sam and Montgomery will be happy grandmas together." If it got too hot, we changed into 1964 bikinis and biked to the local swimming pool in matching magenta shorts and t-shirts over our bathing suits. As we slathered on the baby oil, we dissected the attributes of recent boyfriends and their eligibility for marital consideration. Oh yes, I recognized that address.

I was so excited. Mary Claire knew exactly what I might like as a wedding gift. Eagerly I clipped open the constraining plastic tape with the scissors always at the ready on my desk. Inside there was a small amount of gift wrap and tissue taped awkwardly around what I was sure would be a perfect gift. At least it could have been. The long-stemmed and delicate wine glasses—predictably red, our favorite color—lay in sad shards under the parsimonious paper. My excitement turned to devastation. I swallowed the tears that came. Why hadn't she wrapped these beautiful glasses properly? Mary Claire was always so careful about details. What happened to her? Something must be seriously wrong.

Just the same, I made sure she got an invitation to the wedding. I hoped she'd change her mind. But she did not come. I never saw her again.

Later I heard from another classmate who kept in touch with her that she was indeed diagnosed as anorexic. She had gone into treatment more than once, but even that was an ambivalent gesture. I didn't understand.

Frowning, the classmate told me that Mary Claire always put something heavy into her pockets when the supervisors in the in-patient facility weighed her. She was careful to avoid more than tiny bits of food whenever she could. Somehow she wanted both to get better and to remain very skinny. When she noticed in the mirror that her pelvic bone displayed itself through her unpadded skin, she told herself she needed to lose more weight. She was too fat. She contracted her daily meal portions and did one more mile on the treadmill. Apparently she still survived only on grapefruit and rice cakes, meted out one by one.

As things got worse and she began to realize she was on a path to self-destruction, she panicked and sought help again. It was time to get serious. Back to the hospital. This time she really tried—no pocket rocks or healthy food squirreled under the empty potato peel so no one would see it. Apparently after so many years of deprivation her body became adjusted to her destructive regimen. Now, each time she tried to keep a reasonable portion of healthy food down, her body rejected it. Anorexia chose a lifetime partner: bulimia.

I never found out what happened to her. Did she continue to eat just enough to keep her electrolytes balanced? Did the doctors find a way to help her keep what food she ate where it belonged? I wonder if she kept that unworn bridesmaid dress. It was red. Maybe today it is too small for her. I hope so.

Originally, I wrote this story as a catharsis. Then I began to think that it might be suitable for publication. I printed a copy to read before I sent it off to *The Sun*. The daily crossword was complete, and reading it once more gave me something to do while I tried out the new "gourmet food court" at a local shopping center. I ordered my usual sinful delight—a bit of fortification for the afternoon slump. I settled into a quiet corner. As I bit into the warm deliciousness of my snack, some random red sprinkles scattered on the papers. I thought of Mary Claire. Was she alive somewhere, munching on a warm doughnut? I wondered.

A Trip to the CABG Patch[1]

"Teddy Bear, say goodnight."

PAIN IN MY LEFT arm signaled something wrong with this seventy-something body. The doctor ordered tests. "Take some Ativan before you come," he said, "It will lower your blood pressure." Just four minutes on a treadmill predicted a likely serious heart attack. He stopped the test immediately and ordered a catheterization.

The invasive cardiologist called the day before to reassure me. I would be myself again. My husband had a stent years ago and cleaned the basement drains the next day. I could live with that. I could live.

I chatted briefly with the nurse and entered happy land. Later, the doctor was not smiling. The heart muscle and other vessels looked pretty good (for an old lady, I added to myself), but the major arteries showed a tight community of plaque like that which killed my father at sixty-two. The pictures said it all: bypass.

CABG, they call it, coronary artery bypass graft. I always liked the pungent taste of cruciferous vegetables: cabbage, brussels sprouts, cauliflower. "Cruciferous" has other implications in Christian tradition. Years ago, before a Caesarean section, I remember thinking that the position on the operating table was exactly that of the executed Jesus. This time the "crucifixion" would be more dramatic. And there was no newborn as a prize for participation.

Three days left before surgery. To dissipate my anxiety I cleaned the attic, shoveled snow, returned library books, and finished the manuscript of

1. This story originally was published in *Commonweal*. Used with permission.

19

the book I was writing. With our children, grandchildren, and friends, my husband and I had celebrated fifty years of marriage—two accomplished lovers. The rest of my bucket list could be dumped. It no longer seemed important.

They invaded me with tubes. They stayed the bloody traffic of my heart and rearranged its roadways. They cracked my chest, pumped me with morphine, someone else's blood, lidocaine and lactose, glucose and glue. When I awoke several hours later, the family stood silently at the bedside. Their frowning faces said everything.

Efficient people in white removed tubes, leaving tracks of tape and violated skin. They moved my body—was it still my self?—to a step down room. After two more days they retrieved the remaining wires, captured the damage and repair in ghostly pictures, and pronounced me "discharged." No more sleeping on the back of a sheeted stretching animal that hospitals wrongly call a "bed."

Who came home? Was I the same person, or had she died? The random winter fly in the house was drawn to the cadaverous smell of my personal Golgotha—blood cells congealed on the surgical site. It believed *I* no longer existed. It smelled only "lunch."

Appointments with cardiologist and surgeon followed. The old me would have persisted when these men interrupted my questions with their medical wisdom. Now I felt infantilized, muzzled, and frustrated. I felt diminished when others told me when to walk, what to eat. The doctors dictated what and when pills should be taken.

Although only a small scar remains where they took the left radial artery, I wonder if the complete I will live again, resurrected from the CABG patch? Is there a born again me? There is still a pulse on the right wrist, but—like me—the left is silent. The arteries that nourished six children are misplaced, diverted to supplant crippled heart vessels clogged to worthlessness. Their proper place is silent. The long angry scar down my torso remembers my expiration. Now, like Shakespeare's Caesar, "ripped . . . from his mother's womb," I have been ripped from my natural course toward death. This feels wrong, unnatural.

Maybe there is efficacious work ahead. Survival from surgery, survival not only from the physical pain and mutilation but from the pain I see in the eyes of those who love me. My husband has suffered far more than I. While I was confident of the surgeon's skill, my husband—also a doctor— knew too well the risks and embraced them with the arms of his anxiety.

There is also the work of mourning my old life. Before the surgery I was prepared to die. "Please," I told the surgeon, "If I go sour, let me go. I do not want to live a vegetable life, even as a CABG!" We agreed to the lie that no resuscitation would be attempted in the OR. Every ethicist knows that even clear advance directives are suspended in the surgical suite. But now am I prepared to live?

As the transplanted arteries strain to find new paths in which to grow, perhaps my life will likewise regenerate. A friend sent me a card not long ago. Its message: "There is a time when you believe that everything is finished. That will be the beginning." (Louis L'Amour)

Recovery from the surgery itself was easy. The psychic recovery less so. (When I first wrote this account, I knew little of Louis L'Amour, a man who had reinvented himself many times: mine assessment worker, boxer, merchant seaman, poet, prolific author of novels. Perhaps this is a clue for me.)

Personal dignity and integrity demand that the values of the patient be respected and honored, beyond the limits of HIPPA (the patient privacy law). Between the assault to the body and to his or her intelligence, the patient can be reduced to a thing, a non-responsible biological entity—the heart in Room 3. My children came home to care for me, reprising the family joke of calling me "Honey Badger." Honey Badger don't care!

Vulnerability is the unwelcome companion to any human medical situation. Ethicist Warren Reich proposed it be added to the list of principles of bioethics, an antidote to the unbridled hegemony of autonomy in American medical practice. Deprived of clothes, placed in a situation where one is perceived—sometimes rightly—as less informed, it is difficult to formulate intelligent questions, much less muster the decision-making power required to take control of one's own medical destiny. Reich called for "concerned care" to be substituted for what he names the "desiccated principle of beneficence."

Psychic wounds heal more slowly than physical scars. Many months after the surgery I found myself crying unreasonably about a bruised rib, unrelated to but near the healed sternum. Taken by surprise at the emotional response considerably greater than the bruise required, I insisted to my husband that the new insult must be connected to the bypass. Yet I knew full well that it was not. Patients, and likewise their families, must embrace the pain that is part of human living, part of entering into the sufferings of Christ. The medical system must do more than remind patients of follow-up appointments and embrace eagerly new medicines and new treatments. It must understand the incidence of ongoing trauma from serious affronts to the body that patients feel. These interventions go deeper than scalpel cuts. Like the fading scars on my body, their healing may never be complete.

This narrative above was written eight years ago. Seems as if it never happened, although occasionally I sign e-mails to my children H. B. for Honey Badger. The scars on my chest and wrist are still there, but the trauma of both the surgery and the recovery seem to belong to another person, to another story entirely. Like the angry red of the surgical slices, they have morphed into a distant memory. There is a balm, a mercy in the forgetfulness that time brings. Yet there is a lingering understanding of what it means to be vulnerable, to be at the mercy not only of one's bodily vulnerability—one's genes and behavior—but of the need for others.

A twentieth-century moral thinker, Louis Janssens, developed a series of qualities which define the human person. One of these, mostly ignored by individualistic Americans, is that human beings in their essence cannot escape their bodiliness, the reality that any material and living thing is limited and fading. No miracle pill or vigorous health regime will change that, no matter how convincing television promotion of pills with funny names make claims. We will all grow old and wear our trousers rolled, as T. S. Eliot's Prufrock lamented. We can choose to dissipate limited energies to fight the process. We can use sensible measures to keep fit. In the end, though, all our good intentions and shiny weapons must be laid down in surrender, and finally yielded in death.

Janssens notes that we are inexorably connected to one another, agreeing with John Donne that no man [or woman] is an island. From the time our nascent dripping bodies take a first breath and break into their first cry and even before, we are dependent on the care and kindness of others. Tennessee Williams's character Stella was not the only one who thought this.

As we grow up, we develop the illusion that we set our own course. The rugged individual is the American paradigm. Even the pill pushers tell us to "Go your own way." This is illusion. It is others who till the ground in which our selves take root and grow; others who hold the light to point our path. We do not ourselves build roads or cars or houses to move us along or keep us protected from the elements.

Recently I bought a jump rope. This was not for a regimen of exercise. I thought it might be fun to play the game that was so much the part of childhood fun. I even put it on my bucket list: "One more time jumping rope." When the package came, I tore into it eagerly, to try out my new toy. Sadly, as with so many other discoveries that accompany aging, I discovered that the powers of gravity were intensely stronger than they had been on that St. Wenceslas playground so many years ago. But I will never forget the rhyme:

> Teddy Bear, Teddy Bear, turn around,
> Teddy Bear, Teddy Bear, touch the ground, . . .

At eighty, I can still turn around. Touching the ground takes a bit more doing. Neither of these actions can be done while wielding a colorful clothesline over my head and under my feet. It's time. I must yield my new jump rope to the kids next door. Perhaps they will put down their hand-held device and learn the fun of teasing the teddy. But Teddy Bear, like Honey Badger, has another task awaiting ever more urgently.

> Teddy Bear, Teddy Bear,
> Turn out the light.
> Teddy Bear, Teddy Bear,
> Say good night—one last time.

Hard Choices
in the Garden of Good and Evil

"... when love is in, the wit is out."

(WILLIAM SHAKESPEARE)

I MET HER WHEN she was in her twenties. She and her husband, Bill, bought a home down the street from us on winding Cane Grinder Lane. They were one of many nascent families in our middle-class suburb, having children and framing dreams in cookie cutter new construction beyond the lazy Southern elegance of past eras. Our kids played together, and we took turns driving to Hilton Head for weekend outings. In those *Leave It to Beaver* days, most of us young wives were content to stay home with the children, keep a reasonably clean house, bake an occasional batch of cookies, and read mediocre novels for the neighborhood get-me-out-of-the-house book club. Not so Janet.

Janet was a brilliant woman. Eventually a tenured university professor, she was always active in politics. When she was still in graduate school at Chapel Hill, a young academic struggling to publish her dissertation and achieve a foothold in a male profession, she worked to elect the first black mayor of a southern city. Her books on political theory were favorably reviewed and used as texts all over the country. But that was then.

After she retired, she still enjoyed the monthly lunch with "the girls" (as the women academics called themselves) at a local all-you-can-eat restaurant. Savannah catered to tourists, especially along the water. Locals knew the better places, where the shrimp was fresh and the service impeccable. These lunches were fun for everyone. For the retired women, it punctuated the empty days of retirement bereft of students or the tedious work of class preparation, tests, and grades. They provided a way to catch up on university gossip ("Did you know the head of chemistry was fired for propositioning his secretary?" "I cannot believe they moved the graduate department to that tiny space! Boy, was the dean ticked." "The 'faculty' parking area is getting smaller every year. Must be nice to be 'staff' with all those new spots assigned just to you!"). They encouraged continued thinking and writing, and simply afforded an opportunity to enjoy one another's company. For those still working fulltime, it allowed a forum for airing institutional concerns without consequences or censure.

Many universities were still having trouble viewing women, especially married women, as equal to their male counterparts. Breaking into the college professorial clique was difficult. A numerical minority on the university faculty, these women began their bonding lunches well before tenure. The "boys" generally did their own thing. The sparse cadre of senior women faculty helped young professors integrate into the confusing landscape of academia.

Often the group descended on the restaurant at the same time. Janet usually hitched a ride with one of her mentors, who lived nearby. That professor, someone whom I knew only casually, told me the story. As they entered the restaurant that humid Thursday, a Hispanic woman approached Janet warmly. She lit up and greeted her with hugs. But her colleague saw something else. Janet responded with a smile and a few words, but her eyes betrayed her. They carried a vacant, confused look. She had no idea who this woman was. She was a well-respected judge, another person of color Janet worked diligently to elect.

When she got home from the lunch that day, Janet's mentor called me. I didn't know her all that well, so I was surprised. What was this about? Hesitating, she told me that she was concerned about Janet. Knowing that we were close, Dr. Wagner wondered what I thought. I told her Janet seemed fine to me. We had gone shopping together last week, discussed the latest John Berendt work her book club was reading (we both devoured *Midnight in the Garden of Good and Evil*, when it first came out), and then wound down with wine and cheese before we went our separate ways. Nothing seemed different to me. Oh, maybe she forgot some of the book's details and ordered a different wine from her usual, but nothing much seemed out of the ordinary.

Dr. Wagner continued. Other friends from the university—especially those who knew about her father—increasingly were becoming concerned about Janet. She became the subject of whispered conversation in the faculty lounge. Former colleagues saw hints of memory loss. Increasingly Janet was asking the same questions, returning to the same subjects, several times during a conversation. "How is your new book going? And how are the children?" One of the regulars at the monthly lunch, back from sabbatical doing serious research in Appalachia, was excited to outline her latest project. She detailed with enthusiasm the interviews she had recorded and a well-known publisher's interest. When the conversation lagged a few minutes later, Janet turned to her and asked, "Are you writing anything right now? You must catch me up on your kids." The woman's only offspring were her numerous books.

Next time Janet and I saw each other, she mentioned that she noticed the signs herself. She apologized during conversations, "Did I tell you this already?" Dementia lurked in the corners of her mind. Her dad lived with the disease for ten years before he died. She remembered the vacant stares as the disease progressed. In the mirror she recognized the same faraway look in her own eyes. Increasingly she was sure the demon dementia had resurfaced in her generation. Her concern drew her to see a doctor. A professional could reassure her. But she flunked the memory test.

This news obviously upset her. She protested, perhaps too much. In grade school she remembered even the slightest details of every reading assignment. In high school and college some kids kept a written schedule of when papers were due, and tests were expected. *She* stored all this in the notebook of her brain. When one of her students asked a question in class, Janet could call up five references that addressed it. "Good heavens," she said. "I can still recite the state capitals and that poem about Hannibal that I learned in third grade." She felt a need to recite it to me: "Hannibal crossed the Alps . . . With his black men, his brown men, his countrymen, his town men . . ." She paused. She was almost in tears.

Deep inside, she was forced to embrace the reality. As a college professor who researched everything, as well as from her own experience, she realized also there was little she could do. There was no dam strong enough to restrain the waves that eroded her cognition. They would pound and pound until they breached completely any mental barricades and washed away the sands of now as well as the grains of then. She knew the promising pills advertised on television were neither a panacea nor a cure.

Bill was a constant support during her dad's long progressive illness. Although the father was in Massachusetts (her parents divorced when Janet was fourteen and her dad lived alone), they visited as often as they could. Two years ago her dad fell and broke his leg. The healing took a long time. Janet was in the middle of the semester, so Bill arranged time off from his medical practice to stay with Dad during his recovery. Bill is, as they say, a real mensch.

It became harder and harder to keep track of what was going on with Grandpa. Janet's teaching schedule allowed some extended time during summers to visit and help her father navigate his affairs. Now safely tenured, she need not grind out publication after publication and could spend more time with him. Nevertheless, he *was* in another city and he needed more care than an occasional visit could afford. His memory was slipping. It was time to bring in a live-in care giver. Several candidates were interviewed and vetted. A suitable person was hired. Janet could focus more on her own life. At least for a while.

The last few times she ventured north, Janet noticed items missing from his home. First it was the merino wool sweater they bought him for Christmas. Maybe he didn't like it and gave it away to a charity. He complained that its pockets were not deep enough for him to carry everything. The next time it was a small Hummel figure, a little blue-eyed girl in a babushka dangling her legs from the branch of a blooming apple tree. Maybe it was broken and thrown away. How many times had Janet and Bill seen their energetic Dalmatian whack something into smithereens with his excitable tail? No need to ask about these things. Likely Dad would not remember.

More recently the disappearing items became less breakable and more valuable. Silver goblets engraved with her parents' initials (from their misbegotten marriage), a pearl necklace Janet wore at their wedding (the "something borrowed"), even the cell phone Bill sent him recently ("Fred, it will help you keep in touch") were all gone. Dad didn't seem to notice—or care. Since no one else was in or out of the house besides the father and the care giver, the conclusion was clear. Barring alien kidnappers shopping at Fred's Open Pantry, the care giver must be responsible. Bill suggested they prosecute her, but Janet's dad was not a reliable witness. Likely long-distance police process was not worth the effort. Nonetheless the woman had to be fired. Janet concluded that monitoring from a distance was no longer going to work.

Fortunately, the house to which Janet and Bill moved was much grander than their starter home. It near the center city, not too far from the house in Janet's favorite "local" book. Live oaks dripping with Spanish moss flanked the front lawn. A small carriage house on the commodious property provided the solution to Dad's situation. Dad became a part of their everyday world. No assisted living facility for him.

One last trip to Massachusetts, belongings sorted and sold. Another summer past without leisure or academic creativity. Since Janet was an only child, there was no one else to help or to covet the assorted acquisitions of a long life. An aging quilt, sewn long ago by Janet's paternal grandmother for her little Freddie, was tucked into the car for the final journey south.

Janet and Bill made sure to pack all of Dad's favorite items: the cap from his dress uniform, the souvenir kimono from his year in Japan as World War II was winding down, his class ring engraved with his initials (*FCL*), even a tennis racket, its skeleton warped painfully with age. He did not remember any of them. Janet did.

Among the family pictures she found fragile letters with blacked-out portions, written during her dad's wartime tour of duty. Whenever one arrived her mother opened it hungrily, tearing away the wafer-thin airmail envelopes. She'd read them aloud to her only daughter. The two cried as they comprehended the unspeakable horrors of war. Janet's mom and dad were still in love then.

When he returned from the war, these horrors built a barrier between her parents that was impossible to bridge. A divorce ensued. Janet's mom remarried, moved to Oregon, and died unexpectedly of a ruptured aneurysm. Janet saw no reason to keep in touch with her stepfather.

Although she and her family moved from our suburban neighborhood when the house became too small for their kids, their junk, and Janet's growing professional library. During this painful process of relocating her dad Janet called me almost every day, crying, to decompress the sadness of it all. "Do you know how much stuff a person can collect in a lifetime? He kept forty years of *National Geographic* in the basement. Ye gods! He even sorted them by date! He was never going to read them, although they'd be new to him now! Do you have any idea how hard it is to watch your father lose his memory, his very being?" She tried not to dump on Bill any more than she had to. I was happy to listen.

When they got back to Savannah, Janet forced herself to be upbeat. She could suck it up and sacrifice one precious summer for Dad's safety and comfort. He was installed in the carriage house, his things set in order. The teenage children stepped in to help. Janet sounded a bit more hopeful as she described to me the sun-washed bedroom, the updated kitchen, the cozy fireplace in the living room—wood stacked for a cold winter. For Savannah residents "winter" meant anything colder than forty degrees. Too bad that merino sweater was gone. Although Dad had stayed there whenever he visited Janet, the apartment now was a brand-new experience. Even though he did not quite understand, he seemed pleased.

The family hired a person to come twice a week to cook a few meals, to change linens and keep the small space clean. This time they made sure that she had good references. Close at hand, now, they always knew what was going on. Dad was carefully supervised, well cared for.

At first things seemed better and life returned to normal. But in the second year even this arrangement became insufficient. The dementia thrived. It was time to face the reality. Dad needed more than they were able to give. He was moved to a total care facility. Although they wanted to keep him "at home," his condition was too serious. Janet brought along her grandmother's homemade quilt and some favorite photos. A few familiar items might give him comfort.

This time Janet included a sturdy iron coin bank in the shape of a pug dog. It had a lock on its belly to access its accumulated treasure. Her dad gave it to Janet and Bill shortly after they were married, during one of his visits. They deposited all their spare change into it, per Dad's counsel. They called it their "retirement account." It resembled a deceased family pet, one her father loved very much. Every time her dad came to visit, he would sneak in a few coins. He thought they didn't see. Now they were a long-forgotten memory.

Although he recognized none of them, a member of the family dropped in frequently. Janet came more often, usually every day. Dad complained to her and to anyone who would listen that his daughter never visited. As she told me this, Janet choked back the tears.

In those days she and I had lunch frequently. She continued to need someone besides Bill to whom to vent. We became a fixture at that lovely restaurant. Local grouper and coleslaw. Plenty of white wine and wadded Kleenex on the side.

Then Dad was gone. Janet's children were grown and scattered to other states. All but one of them lived a very generous drive away. The "close" one lived down in Jacksonville! Janet and Bill were alone, and now she was re-capitulating her father's journey. Knowing and dreading what was to come, Bill assumed her care, reluctance mitigated by abiding love. I called her from time to time, but the occasions were less frequent and more painful. I realized that she no longer knew who I was. The disease was progressing, an ironic recapitulation of all she went through with her dad.

Janet knew the symptoms. In the beginning she took careful notes of family names, important dates, which former colleagues came to last month's lunch, any information that might help her remember things. She labeled the cupboards with what was kept in them and put a bright red hook near the back door. It would jar her memory as to where she kept the car keys. Soon, however, she didn't need the keys any longer. Even driving familiar streets for a short time, she got lost frequently. Thank God for cell phones!

Bill contracted his medical practice to care for Janet. He did everything to support her. He made sure she had a ride to the monthly luncheons with the girls. He marked her coats, gloves, and umbrella—rain was unpredictable in Savannah—with her name and address. She tended to leave them wherever she went. He protected her from embarrassment whenever he could by announcing the name and context for someone they met by chance at church, out to dinner, or just on a walk around the city. Savannah has such lovely public spaces.

Then there came the night Janet woke, confused and frightened. She yelled at Bill. "What are you doing in my bed?" She no longer recognized the father of her children—all of whom bore his curly black hair and pleasant smile. He tried to reassure her. For the moment, for that first time, that reassurance worked. They went peacefully to sleep, warm in each other's arms.

Later, reassurance did not help. Increasingly frightened at the sight of a "stranger" in her bedroom, she banished him to the bunk beds now empty of grown children. "You are not my husband!" No matter what he said or did, she did not know the man she had *known* so many times. It was time again to select a nursing home. In the end, they chose the place where her father had died. Evening Angels welcomed another resident.

At first Bill visited frequently. He made sure her room decor included that patchwork quilt retrieved after her father's death. Its pieced-together patches, fabric from grandma's many sewing projects and full of their own stories, were beginning finally to fade, to fray, and to rip apart from each other. Some of the patches were wool. Tiny moth holes interrupted the lovely red and green plaid pattern that defined Fred's Irish heritage. The quilt was a sober metaphor for the family curse.

I visited once or twice, mostly out of guilt. Favorite books lined the shelves, although Janet no longer read political philosophy—or even the few novels that she never gave away. I noticed her copy of *Midnight in the Garden of Good and Evil*. I wondered if she remembered walking by the house.

Framed family smiled lovingly at her from the shelf above the small desk. She saw strangers. Still, she and Bill enjoyed the parties that Evening Angels provided for its residents. She flirted with this "new" person each time he came. Sitting on the bedside table in her room was a picture of the two of them, arm in arm at the home's New Year's Eve gala. Local shrimp were piled in abundance on their plates and the ice-cold punch flowed freely.

Poor Bill. Even when he was with her, he missed her so much. He was very lonely. We invited him over for dinner from time to time, but it was not enough.

Then, one day when he was fooling around on the computer on an older-singles site, he met Elaine. Everything he read seemed to fit. She was a widow and retired teacher. She was funny, alive, engaging. She appreciated the same vintage movies that Bill loved. They had so much in common. Both enjoyed the yearly Irish parade that marked Savannah's early heritage. The celebration lasted nearly a month, beginning with the Irish Festival in February and culminating on St. Patrick's Day a month later. For that whole month Elaine and Bill spent nearly all their time together, often at the various Irish functions. They watched the fountain in Forsyth Park take on Irish green and cheered at the parade. They laughed, stopped for a craft beer and some oysters, held hands like kids with a high school crush. At night they yearned to lay exhausted in the same bed.

The ache in Bill's heart lessened, as did his visits to Evening Angels. The relationship between Bill and Elaine grew. They began to talk about the future. Janet seemed content as she was, and she did not recognize Bill as her husband. Soon the disease would claim her life, but what about the now?

Bill had always taken his marriage vows seriously, at least until he met Elaine. What should he do now? The children were divided: two were angry about the relationship, believing he had betrayed their mother; the others were more understanding. They thought that their dad deserved to be happy. After all, he had done his best for Janet. Now it was time to do something for himself.

One more issue complicated the decision. Bill and Janet were devoted Catholics. Each Sunday when the kids were little, the whole family sat in the front row of the Savannah cathedral. It was only a short walk from the lovely Victorian home with the carriage house. Although Janet had her full-time job, she taught Sunday School to small children each week after Mass. Bill walked the kids home and prepared breakfast. His connection to church and charity was less pious than it was practical.

The Catholic faith teaches that marriage is "until death do you part." There seemed to be no exception for those whose spouse no longer knew them. Bill felt some qualms about his relationship with Elaine, but he brushed those away. The comfort he got from Elaine was justified, given how much he had sacrificed for Janet. In the end, they decided. It was time.

Janet's former colleagues continue to gather for their monthly lunch. Now they have new stories to share, and the gossip has little to do with the university.

Please!

"We shout and scream and wail and cry, but in the end we must all die."

(MR. CARSON, *DOWNTON ABBEY*)

TODAY THE PAIN WAS in charge. Mom asked me to drive carefully. As I helped her into the car, every move evoked a slight gasp. We took it slowly, but clearly she was not comfortable. She melted gently into the passenger seat and sighed with relief. We were on our way.

Drops of morning dew lingered on the trees and sidewalks. Silence and a sense of dread hung between us as we navigated suburban streets toward the sterile office building. Anxiety easily short-circuits conversation. As a distraction, I turned on the radio just in time to hear a commercial about a hospital that specialized in cancer treatment. Just what I needed!

After what seemed like an eternity, we reached the asphalt expanse of the parking lot. It was early morning. Thankfully we found a space near the door. Every time we suggested it, Mom refused to get a handicap sticker. "That's for challenged people, Susan. And besides, you are the one who drives me." I swallowed my anger. The asphalt chasm between any parking space and the building seemed to increase each time we made this trip. I engineered her carefully from the car. Slowly we overcame the distance to the door.

Assuming we were unfamiliar with the place—really?—the perky lime-jacketed volunteer at the desk directed us to "Doctor's office" on the third floor. How many times had we come and gone to this place where bad news flourished like an unwanted weed? Good news, not good directions, was the response we hoped for. What did the last batch of tests show? Was the treatment working? Was there anything more we should consider?

The waiting room was almost empty. One man sat unobtrusively in a corner chair, near the bubbling tank filled with calico fish designed to soothe fearful patients. The man shifted in his seat. Tired magazines sprawled on the tiny table. Impatient, the man kept looking at his watch. "When is it going to be time? I'm been sitting here forever."

Apparently our appointment preceded his. Just after we settled into the boring beige chairs (certainly not conducive to the predictable long waits) and began to page through dog-eared issues of *People*, the secretary called my mother. "Ann, *Doctor* is ready to see you." (Why can't they use an article! He is *the* doctor. That's not his name! And why don't they call Mom by her last name? She deserves that respect. After all, she's old—and seriously ill!) "Ann" eased up slowly from her chair and went in alone. I looked away from the frowning guy in the corner. *People* suddenly became seductively interesting.

Just ten minutes later, "Doctor" came into the waiting room. Her face said it all. It *was* time. Increased pain proved an accurate harbinger. The cancer mushrooming throughout Ann's body signaled that death's door would open in a few months, maybe sooner. Tests indicated that the disease was progressing rapidly. The doctor remarked that it was fortunate that Mom had suffered no broken bones as the cancer spread. "But there's nothing more we can do."

We knew for a long time that no matter how aggressively medical intervention was applied, the cancer was determined to take Mom's life. She and I talked about her final days often. The plan was to keep her at home, and comfortable. That was what she wanted. After a long career as a visiting nurse, she knew how much better people did in their own homes. But this day of death sentence arrived much too soon. The "when" became a "now." We were in shock as we left. The receptionist handed us a small business card with the information about choices for our next step.

I told Mom to wait until I got the car. She insisted on walking back with me. "They're giving up on me, aren't they? They don't care." She looked stunned, although she had to know the prognosis for her disease. Even so, she did not want to face it. Didn't all the obituaries describe how everyone "battles" cancer to the very end? I, too, felt defeated, angry; but I couldn't let Mom see that. *Suck it up, Susan. Suck it up.*

As soon as we arrived home and Mom got settled, I called hospice. The response was quick and efficient. They could start right away. A nurse came to assess Mom's situation and needs. The dread reality sunk in: less than six months and she would be gone.

The hospice team began to come each week to provide supportive services and symptom control. The savvy nurse managed to charm her reluctant patient into taking pain medication, but only if she cut the pill in half. Absent this veteran care giver, though, Mom rarely took any medication. As a retired nurse she knew the possible side effects of serious pain drugs. She probably knew too much. She witnessed addiction and how the body developed an increased "taste" for those seductive pills. She wanted to be in charge, mind alert at all times. The plastic prescription bottle kept sentinel at the bedside—soldier at the ready—but its potent weapons were rarely discharged. Occasionally the pain pushed aside Mom's reluctance, but most of the time she just gritted her teeth, smiled, and refused. She wanted the support of all her faculties, even as the pain tempted her resolve.

With hospice support, we were confident she could manage on her own. We hoped. We were wrong. Her stamina diminished more rapidly than before. Larry, my younger brother, moved in. After work he cooked supper, helped Mom bathe, and was there at night if she awoke.

I tried to help, but care giving is not my gift. Even so, I pitched in when needed. I called every day when Larry was not available and brought Mom's favorite chocolate globs from the local bakery, whenever I could. She enjoyed a cup of tea and a cookie, a bit of social interaction for a short time with both of us, before she went to bed. One evening Larry and I raised gently the idea of getting an alert system, just in case. Mom vehemently declined those charm-like monitors that hang around the neck. No extra jewelry for her! I told myself it was fine. *It's all good. It will be only six months at the longest.* I took another bite of the chocolate glob (and wished for red wine).

Mom was always fiercely independent. In those slim-budget days, we had had only one car. When Dad was at work, Mom and I were dependent on public transportation. Unfortunately, the suburban bus did not run all the way to our house.

One morning, just a month before Larry was born, we planned a whole day downtown. We anticipated a leisurely brunch, shopping at the three department stores (pre-Amazon) that lined the main street, and the new Disney movie with popcorn (extra-large). Before he left for work, Dad drove us to the bus stop. He promised to pick us up on his way home from the office, but he sometimes ran late (meetings, meetings, meetings). This was one of those times.

We waited for nearly thirty minutes at the bus stop. It was windy and snowing. Mom grew increasingly impatient. She was hungry, Larry was kicking, and I had to go to the bathroom. Angrily she gathered her packages, and me; and we started walking at a brisk pace the two miles to our house. I was only about four, but I was determined to keep up with Mom's pace.

It was beginning to get dark. About ten minutes into the walk a police car spotted us and stopped. Mom assured him that we could manage without his help. The officer offered, no insisted, that he drive us home. (I was delighted, given the urgency of my problem.) That was then. Hopefully, her pregnant determination would get her through this final journey as well.

Even with the increasing pain and ebbing energy, Mom still got around the house. She generally microwaved a lunch of leftovers from Larry's culinary efforts (he's a pretty good cook) and looked forward to his nightly return. Most of the day she read or watched TV. Old *Mash* episodes held up well. The dialogue was still great: full of puns, except for the occasional break-up of the old tapes—a bit like Mom. And many of the cast have died, a bit like . . . oh, it's so hard!

Gradually Mom became unable to get out of bed, even with help. She slept more during the day and seemed to be in greater discomfort. The hospice team could not be there all the time. We hired a daytime care giver. It was expensive, but it was essential. The mounting cost beyond the in-home hospice began to nag more and more incessantly. Although ambivalent about my feelings, I hoped it would soon be over.

Larry's tenure as night nurse ended much too soon. A young lawyer, he had serious school debt. The firm where he worked offered him a position on the west coast. He could not refuse such a promotion: more money and a step up in the firm. I must admit I was angry as I said my goodbyes at the airport.

Although I have a decent job, after the divorce I still struggled to pay my bills. Taking more time from work was not an easy option. I was really upset at Larry's seemingly easy decision to leave, but what could I do? Besides, as the older, I was the unofficial PIC (person in charge). "Susan, watch your brother while I go to the store. Susan, please take out the hamburger for dinner. Susan!" I still hear those responsibility words playing in my head.

I sighed and packed a small bag, resigned to spend the nights with Mom. I had no choice. Carla was available only in the mornings. Hospice visits were scheduled only once a week. It was going to be tough.

One night shortly after Larry's departure Mom had an episode. It was around three in the morning. It looked as if it was time. From what the hospice folks told me to expect, she seemed to be actively dying. Her advance directives made it clear that no rescue squad should be allowed to arrest the process, but I was sure she would want a priest. I looked in on her frequently, waited two more hours, and then called Father Martin, a family friend. He always had early Mass, so I knew he was up by then. He came right after Mass was over. His homily that morning was unusually short!

By the time he arrived, Mom had settled down and seemed a bit better. He sighed onto the kitchen chair, waiting for her to wake. Poor Father Martin! His eyelids drooped from time to time. Gratefully he accepted a cup of coffee—high test. Rising so early every day demanded a brief nap mid-morning. Today's news deprived him of that modest luxury. The coffee would have to do.

Trying to make small talk as he warmed his hands around the cup, he commented on the bulletin board on the kitchen wall. Chocked full of family photos, most of them curling at the edges, it chronicled the growth and development of our family. Pictures of us from babyhood to the time Mom put away her camera for good. That was right after Dad died.

I love the one just after the snowball fight, Larry and I snow-covered and smiling. We were flanked between the snowman we had built and the six-foot magnolia, bare in the winter cold. That magnolia is now as tall as the house and commands the front yard. Mom had gone in to get her ever ready camera. The snowball hit me hard a minute before she reappeared to capture the scene on film. Larry quickly wiped his nose, dripping blood from my retaliatory punch, and smiled for the camera. We laughed about it later.

Father Martin administered the last rites, chatted briefly with Mom, and left for his now-cold bed. The daytime care giver, Carla, was on time as usual. She arrived consistently just before Mom woke, to help her with the morning routine.

But Mom lingered on. And then things got even worse. Frightening dreams began to punctuate Mom's sleep, disturbing her several times each night. Once she dreamed that Larry had died and that she was somehow responsible for his death. The dream was vivid and frightening, the kind that alerts adrenaline and wakes one in a cold sweat. She pictured an accident. Snow and ice on the road. Sliding into a ditch. Death coming instantly. Larry lay frozen and still at the side of the road, covered in blood—hers. I tried to calm her, but the adrenaline was running. Her terror didn't help my sleep either.

The cold breath of death seemed increasingly to invade every corner of the family house. Each night I shivered as I crawled, exhausted, into bed. The symptoms and the stress became so bad that Mom could no longer be kept at home. It was time for respite care in a situation where her pain could be better managed.

I urged Mom to accept the transfer to in-patient hospice, "at least for the time being." Perhaps the staff there would find a way to keep her comfortable. Clearly the weekly hospice home visit from the cajoling nurse was the only lifeline to comfort she had been willing to grasp, and it was not enough. Perhaps her death was not too far off. I dreaded the idea, but still I hoped. The sooner the better.

The in-patient team mobilized to address the multi-dimensional concerns, doing their job with compassion. Mom continued to resist taking strong medication. She allowed minor palliation but struggled to stay lucid and refused anything that made her sleepy. Her pain became brighter and brighter, causing her awareness to fade into gray. As she weakened and the voice of her concerned daughter demanding stronger pain relief grew louder, it grew more and more difficult for the care team to know how to proceed. They wanted to honor my mother's decisions. I wanted her to be at peace.

For a few hours each night after work I kept vigil at Mom's bed. Nights were still. Drowsing in the tenebrous hospice room, I heard her moan in her sleep. The cancer, now in control of her whole body, fed eagerly on every available organ. The pain got worse. Surely Mom would want relief. But she could no longer articulate her wants. I had to take charge. The hospice staff better listen to *me* now.

First, we had an informal meeting with the care team. The head nurse reiterated that the goal of hospice is to relieve suffering, to promote quality of life *consistent with patient's goals* (emphasis: hers), and to bring comfort to the dying person, the care givers, and family. The treatment plan for Mom as she became weaker was to titrate the medications in such a way that she remained comfortable but stayed awake as much as possible. Complicating choice and dose of medicine were her clear statements that she did not want her mind compromised, did not want to be "foggy." But wasn't she foggy anyway, as the pain increased?

The team tried a variety of new drugs. The first made their patient nauseated. Anyone who has ever been pregnant can identify with the awful feeling of discomfort and malaise. Nausea made a treaty with the pain to share domination of the body. They reveled in their shared hegemony.

Other drugs not expected to cause nausea were started. It would take a few days for them to achieve optimum effect. The nurses and the team doctor visited the patient frequently to make certain that she received what she needed. They continued to seek a balance between symptom relief and doses that would compromise Mom's mind. Nothing seemed to do the job.

I told the hospice people that Mom and I had that serious conversation about her ambivalence and that I had some suggestions. With what I took for condescension, the nurse reminded me: "Now Susan, you know your mom wanted to be aware as long as she could. Medication dulls awareness. She was clear that she did not want to be like people dying in nursing homes, shackled in a cloudy world of drugs between life and death. We try always to respect our patients' *clear* choices."

Yeah, yeah. I turned off her words. *Don't you tell me what my mother wants now*, I thought. I did not want to hear any of this. Hoping to avoid that conundrum, I kept telling myself that death would claim Mom's life soon, the way the cancer now ruled her body in its repressive realm of suffering. Then it would be over. But more time passed, and it wasn't over! It wasn't! Too much. Too much. "You have to do more!" Tears of anger welled.

For me, the quotidian vigil became more and more difficult. I was impatient with the waiting. "Why is it taking so long?" Something must be done. Grasping for anything that might help Mom, I went online to search for a solution. An article, "The Role of Terminal Sedation," several years old, sounded like it had the answer. Terminal sedation relieves pain, but it also suppresses consciousness. If not reversed—that was a possible choice—the patient will never wake up.

Ironically, even without this intervention, Mom's courageous battle to keep control would be lost to the insidious conqueror itself: the pain. People worry that terminal sedation hastens death. The article said it did not. I reasoned that, because it increased comfort, it might give Mom a modest scrap more of life. But was this life?

Hospice administrators believed it was time for an ethics consult. The personnel involved with the case assembled. Other available members of the committee joined by Skype. I was invited to the first part of the meeting. Everyone looked somber. Perhaps the hospice team expected angry confrontation. I was determined to remain calm, though my hands shook and my stomach churned. I expressed my concern that Mom was emotionally and physically in pain. It was clear that Mom, if she were able to express her own wishes, would want this prolonged ordeal over. I let the committee know in not-so-veiled terms that I planned to move my mother, if the home did not agree to my request. It was a reasonable request. I tried to say it gently.

I demanded (well, I probably should not have raised my voice) that Mom be given the "terminal sedation" I read about in the article. I emphasized the "terminal." The hospice staff was not so sure. Was this euthanasia? Someone commented that my mother had left no written confirmation of such a wish. Her deteriorating condition made it difficult for the hospice staff to confirm my assertion, particularly with Mom's persistent refusal of pain medication. But it was obvious to them that I was near my emotional limit.

Would this intervention require artificial feeding? The committee had the advance directive. It stated that she never was to be fed or hydrated artificially. She had typed this in all caps! If this new "comfort measure" lengthened her life and she could not eat or drink on her own, would this require artificial feeding?

They asked what Larry thought. They were afraid that the lawyer in the family might bring charges. But I was the older one. I was the one here! My decision should be honored. I heard someone—was it the ethicist?—make a side comment that there was always that relative in California whose guilt made them want to do everything. They were the ones that sue. Her neighbor chuckled. That made me even angrier.

In the end I'm afraid I made quite a scene. The lid jettisoned from my feelings. "I'm the person in charge. I'm the one who stayed, who saw Mom hurt so badly as her person ebbed away in front of my eyes. Who are you people to make the decision?" I stormed out. The conference continued without me.

To be fair, the team had listened carefully to my plea, but they did not seem convinced that terminal sedation was the way to go. Good care of the dying embraces symptom control: reduction of pain, tempering any side

effects from potent medication, constant presence for the emotional needs
of both the patient and the family. Nevertheless, the request for palliative
sedation, the term used more recently than in the article I referenced, raised
a new and troubling issue for them. What to do?

As I stormed down the hall, a nurse in whom I confided stopped me.
She said she wanted to apologize. Looking rather sheepish, she said that
probably consideration of financial issues muddied the problem for the
people still talking about the case. She told someone on the committee this
information earlier in the day.

Money was on my mind, of course. Time lost from work, the emotional burden of visiting a dying relative, costs that hospice did not cover—
these always added up for family members. But that was not the reason I
asked for terminal sedation! Why didn't they ask me that in the meeting?
Why would I do that? The notion that this concern motivated my request to
hasten Mom's death was *not* true! It was not about the money!

Ethics committees do not dictate decisions; but in this case was my
requesting something that was not within the moral, or maybe legal realm,
the purview of the hospice staff? I thought about all the things I should not
have said. This was not going well. I hoped they might change their minds.
I had done what I could do.

(The team tried to discuss the substantive treatment issues as well as
the emotional distress of everyone concerned. Care givers, particularly ones
that are with patients on an ongoing basis, feel this deeply. The meeting
progressed. Did the daughter really articulate her mother's stated wishes,
or was her motive to have her mother dead? Was it legal or even moral
to administer what she requested? A few of the members had to excuse
themselves. Something must be decided.)

After I stormed out of the conference room, I rehearsed my decision.
Yes. It was time. I knew in that deep lonely place within me that I could live
with the choice I proposed. Father Martin, hospice, even Larry could not
enter there. Certainly the hospice team's goal was the same as mine! I was
sure that Mom could live with it, too. Then I laughed at the irony of what I
had just thought.

It was growing dark. I walked alone down the narrow, shadowy hall.
The white light of winter's death indicated the glass door exit. I pushed its
heaviness into wind and falling snow. The harsh weather bent the barren

bushes of sleeping trees downward. I felt heavy with all the things for which I was responsible. The car looked forlorn in the after-hours parking lot. I shivered. It knew it was not the outside chill but the overwhelming dread of all that was to come.

Aging

Let's Be Frank: Don't Get Old

"Rage, rage, against the dying of the light."

(DYLAN THOMAS)

THEY CALLED HIM "FRANCIS" at the funeral Mass. That was never his name. Frank Cirino Liotta was born in 1907, the oldest of a large Italian family. Cirino was for his father, originally a blacksmith who came to America to make a good life for his family.

When my Dad was fifty, he began to caution, "Don't get old." In the next decade he repeated this mantra with increasing frequency. He had an aversion to sickness or aging. For him they signified moral defect—visible scars of a judgmental plague visited on an unwary body. My father believed in the biblical concept of illness as divine retribution and death as punishment for sin. It was about the only religious idea he embraced.

Frank could not even discuss a subject like death. Once he told our oldest son that a sprawling grassy cemetery they drove past one day was a golf course. I questioned Dad about this obvious lie. His dismissive response: "He's too young to think about such things." Better to paint over death's cold white monuments with warmer golf-course green—if only in denial.

Dad's diligence to maintain his own health was unyielding. He was years ahead of the marathon and yoga generation. Exercise keeps you healthy to a pleasant old age: basketball, swimming, handball, and especially a twice-weekly round of golf. Any kind of physical activity provides protection from those shadowy death-seeking predators that lurk over the body.

He worried about everything from his thinning hair to the remote possibility that his daughter might have a deformed or challenged child. As a young man he read somewhere that wearing hats contributes to baldness, so he never wore a hat. (His hair fell out anyway. Follicles are fickle!)

As to the second concern, he admonished me after our oldest child— a son—was born: "OK, you have a healthy child. That's enough. It's time. Stop." Subtext: another pregnancy might tempt the gods. Perhaps they might send a challenged child. Dad's youngest sister suffered several miscarriages. One—the boy she sought after three daughters—ended in an aborted mole pregnancy.

Frank could not bear such a sorrow for his darling only daughter. He was determined that neither he nor his kin would ever inherit Adam's tainted gene. When our second child was born, it was, "OK. Now you have a boy *and* a girl. It's time. Stop." He lived long enough to see two more healthy grandchildren born. But he never got to teach them golf or how to shoot a basket. He never met their younger siblings.

Sadly, I learned from the same playbook. Repress such things and they will go away. Frank was a good teacher. Sometime in seventh grade I tried to ignore the deep ache in my calves. "I must have run too much yesterday." But when it hurt every time I attempted to raise my leg to step over a three-inch curb, I knew it must be more. Eventually I told my parents.

The doctor made a house call. (They did that in those medieval medical days.) He prescribed a week of bed rest. Later Dad told me I "almost had" scarlet fever. In hindsight the soberness on the faces of both the doctor and my parents suggested that the "almost" of my father's narrative was really "already." Dad simply could not name something that serious in connection to his daughter. Even my brutally honest mother ceded her truth to his fiction.

Glasses? No, I did not need glasses. The cautionary tale in the common culture, "Boys seldom make passes . . ." was sufficient reason to deny my myopia. But the myopia I embraced about my evident condition had more to do with the expected condemnation from Dad. Obliviousness to the tiny branches on distant trees and constant squinting in order to see the blackboard were small prices to pay. I was smart enough to get by, most of the time. While I waited in line for my turn, it was easy to memorize most of the chart used to screen student vision each year. But "most" did not work forever. When the school nurse sent home the unfavorable results of the eye chart test, I "lost" the note before it got there. Then they sent someone to our house. The jig was up. The date for the eye doctor's appointment was made. I cried a lot. And rarely wore the glasses prescribed.

The lessons of childhood are hard to discard. We know that wearing our rubbers—*double entendre* notwithstanding—is not foolproof protection from disease. We know that eating veggies does not grow hair on manly chests, nor does avoiding masturbation keep manly palms hirsute free. Lying does not cause noses to increase in size; truth does not always set one free. Yet such myths persist in our superegos.

I learned and practiced Dad's mantra. If one wants to be "good" it is essential to strive for health. To be ill is to incur moral fault. These insidious tapes play softly on a loop somewhere in my psyche—the quotidian dividend from a high-yield stock.

While I smile when I remember Dad's aversion to illness and dying, I realize it was willed to me: an unwanted inheritance, much like his proffered genes for hypertension. A slight change in blood pressure or laboratory tests, a medical suggestion to take more pills or consider some intervention still render me depressed, defensive, and downright paranoid. It is a matter of pride to keep my weight down, to exercise regularly, to eat vegetables. Fortunately, I enjoy all three.

For most of my increasing years I have been healthy. Yet obsolescence comes even to those who take good care. Bodies lose their mojo. Loud creaks announce the disengagement from a comfortable chair. Skin that shined with youth and vigor takes on the patina of seersucker, and its puckers do no respond to a hot iron—or to a "restoring" cream. Teeth tended with inordinate care begin to fail. Even mountains of medication cannot stave off aging forever.

Luckier than most, chronic aches and the daily ingestion of three cute little pills—priced at the cost of saffron shreds—have little effect on my daily routine. I write, make beds and dinner, lunch with friends, lurch into battle to extricate the weeds from the wheat (in my case daffodils), walk resolutely if reluctantly to the drug store to fetch prescriptions to corral errant blood pressure.

Reluctantly, ice skating and leaping tall buildings with a single bound are crossed off the bucket list. Still, I *can* walk, though now the only path ahead is a direct line toward the door marked "fourth age." A song popular in my youth asked the question, "What's behind the green door?" In the song there's laughter, "hot piano," and "hospitality." The singer wants to go in but is barred. By contrast, the entrance to the faded door to old age gapes wide and beckons like a seductive siren. Likely no hot piano or the hospitality of hot young guys waits inside.

If a person lives long enough, that threshold must be crossed. Sometime around eighty, as it will be soon with climate change, it is too late for healthy habits, medicine, or surgery to resist the ravages of age. Intake of pills increases. Trips to the doctor become a recurrent reminder on the calendar, hospitals become the new iPod hot spots drawing declining devotees with greater frequency. And those sterile accommodations sooner or later end in death.

Chronic illness abuses the aging body with increasing vigor. Tiny chromosomal telemeres, which for so many years rested into recovery during sleep, begin to fail and fall off. Pills promise reversal or "cure," but they receive no passing grade in real life. Inevitably they all lead only to "passing." Interventions may slow the trip to the door to the fourth age; they cannot divert it.

I watched our elderly Weimaraner begin to show telltale aging doggy signs. He lost interest in taunting the squirrels that populated our yard, messing with his hunter-dog head. His fuzzy muzzle turned white and he developed bumps on his sleek silver skin. Although not cancerous, they grew larger and deeper. Less visible growths began to block his urethra. The when and where of his urine stream became less and less under his control. No matter how hard he tried, he found it difficult to navigate the slight step into the backyard to do his thing. The vet confirmed that surgery could remove the blockage, but Captain was too old for that option. Finally, we had him—as they say—put to sleep.

For human beings, the solution is more complicated. Day after day we live with the aches and pains of age. Sleep suspends those feelings, but it is not permanent. We wake to wade into the day through the molasses of failing parts that scream and function like neglected gears bereft of oil. Unlike the failing Weimaraner, we are expected—with due respect to William Shakespeare—to "go gentle into that good night." We cede a home of many years, retain only the fragments of social life: funerals of friends and "special" activities for old people. We retire into anonymity, watching even our memories crumble like the pressed petals of forgotten corsages in a high school scrapbook.

Not only do the elderly struggle to keep up physically or mentally, often they are set aside as burdens too heavy to carry. The face of a daughter-in-law or daughter telling grandma one more time to stand up straight or remember her gloves says it all: exhaustion and frustration screaming from the caring one. It is hard—sometimes heroic—to care for the elderly. But then the understudy takes on the role herself: she *is* the elderly. Pogo had it right!

What to do? Should human beings have the same easy fate as pets? Do animal rights coalesce into the rights of people to decide their own fate? Can human autonomy be invoked to end one's own life, or trump a duty to care for it? Should we counsel the elderly to end vacant lives that consist only of counting the pills, the cost of care, and the meager days left before they die a natural death? Maybe the premise of the 1973 movie, *Soylent Green*, to become food for others, is a proper choice. Or is it better to sustain human shelf life until some celestial use-by date arrives?

Fear as well as phantom hopes can evaporate in the morning mist of a golf course. On Monday of the last week of his life, Frank went out to play his favorite game. He missed the ball off the tee—a mortal sin in golf. He returned home, depressed. His heart disease and general slowing down diminished his capacity. He was no longer the competent golfer whose several trophies testified to his skills. A massive heart attack claimed his life two days later. He died on the porch protected by screens he built with carpentry skill. He was sixty-two.

Was his life cut short too soon? Certainly, but he always lived the years he had with gusto and generosity. His admonition expressed his view of life: "Don't get old." Frank never did.

Interview with Ivy

"Today you are you! That is truer than true!
There is no one alive who is you-er than you!"

(DR. SEUSS)

I was nervous. My university was conducting a study. The goal was to assess preferences of aging adults as to how they wished to live out their lives. Would they rather enter a continuous care facility or remain in their own homes with supportive measures? We students were the "field unit," gathering narratives from real people about their projected choices. What might ideal senior care look like in the future? Our professor hoped to write a book, and perhaps influence how senior care was funded. As the baby boom generation aged, the cost of care was approaching another boom: unmanageable.

The house was in a lovely neighborhood. It was umbrellaed with mature maples just in bud, marching in order on wide tree lawns. Some were gnarled or stretched toward more sun, their girth shaded by trees planted long ago by residents. Others appeared tired, decayed, or carrying the scars of broken branches removed over time. Most of these supported a progressing growth of ivy and abandoned their hope for a longer life. There were some small trees on the tree lawns—flowering pears, an occasional oak— likely replacing trees taken down by the city. I remember reading about a plague of ash borers that decimated many vulnerable trees in this aging ring suburb. In a few places the ground was ravaged and raw, bubbling with wood chips generated from the mangled roots of recently removed trees.

I checked the address and stopped at a lovely colonial. Its trees were young and healthy; straight and beautiful: two dogwoods, upper branches entwined. They were in full bloom, blatant in their defiance of the frigid spring day. I shivered as I locked the car. I looked at my watch. My appointment was for ten. It was time.

It was hard to believe that this sturdy brick housed only two people. It was large, probably with three floors. I had grown up in a similar house—six bedrooms to accommodate our orthodox Catholic family (five children; no birth control). When I—the youngest—left for college, my parents decided to move. The cost and energy of upkeep for such a large property was traded for the secure one-floor condo near public transportation and with a golf-course view. They portioned out our collected detritus, donating what we did not want or did not need (most of it!) to a local charity. Mom complained that we should all covet the treasures she saved so meticulously. Although I fully understood their reasons for moving, at the time I felt tossed out on the street. Dad died soon after the move; Mom three months later. I had no secure place of memory, a familiar wailing wall, a comfort place to grieve.

But today I had another task. Time to put aside my own memories. Time for the interview. I gathered pen and pad, made sure the car was locked, and walked up the drive.

The sign on the front door counseled, "Please knock. Doorbell does not work." Someone had drawn a smiley face on the note. Trained to be obedient, I followed the instructions. The door opened. Ivy was short, looking younger than her seventy-eight years. She was dressed in well-fitting jeans and a cabled turtleneck—no "mom pants" or I "heart" grandma sweatshirt. She invited me into the warm living room. Mid-century furniture appeared recently recovered. (I prefer the Ikea look myself.) The fireplace was blazing with fresh logs, certainly placed just minutes before my arrival. Ivy anticipated how cold her visitor might be. A salt and pepper spaniel splayed out in front of the warmth. He looked up for a moment and then resumed his grand work of the day: a long nap.

My task was to probe the life and particularly the bucket list of this septuagenarian, one of my twenty-five required interviews. I moved a plump pillow to the side and settled nervously on the sofa. Mrs. R. chose the wingback chair. She told me later it was her mother's favorite. Did I want a cup of coffee? Her husband had made biscotti last week, some was still available to go with a hot drink. They had been married for over fifty years. He was semi-retired. Today he was having lunch with a friend. We could have our conversation uninterrupted.

She seemed eager to talk and appeared pretty with-it for an old lady. I am always nervous in these interviews. Sometimes the subjects exhibit memory loss, repeating the same stories again and again. Also, I'm never sure whether I'm pushing too hard. The subject matter is awkward. Talking about aging and death seems tantamount to using four letter words—not ready for prime-time conversation. I sighed, opened my notebook, and began.

Ivy—may I call you Ivy?—how long have you and your husband lived here? They moved here from their starter home one year after the death of her father. As the family grew they needed more space. And it was closer to her mom, who then lived only ten minutes away. Ivy's family could check in on Grandma, invite her over for family dinners, and provide a social life within their household. Her mother did not drive nor was she particularly friendly with her neighbors. Ivy's family provided a respite from total isolation, from lack of human contact except television and the daily paper.

Although she did not appear forgetful, it was not easy to get Ivy to focus. She described in midrashic detail the death of her dad at age fifty-seven (he was struck by lightning). They were such good friends. When Ivy was a girl, they often went to lunch together. They frequented restaurants where he knew the owners. She learned people skills from watching her gregarious dad interact with gangsters, golf buddies, and even grandiose people who lived in gated suburbs and drove Cadillacs.

When she married, her dad transferred his wander lust to Ivy's older children, swooping in from time to time to treat them to lunch. "You need a break," he'd say to her. The kids were returned home, hands clutching small gifts purchased after lunch ("I couldn't say no. He really wanted that toy!") and with faces and clothing slathered with chocolate ice cream.

Ivy pressed on. Like a present-day ancient mariner, she needed to tell me more. "We have been in this house for over fifty years. My dad would have loved it. He always drove down this street and admired the homes, 'built to last.' He pointed out several, the work of a contractor friend. And he always remarked about the trees. My dad loved trees. My parents' lawn— back and front—was all trees! After he died and the city needed to remove some for a new highway ramp, they paid Mom for them. That was great. Dad left only a small estate. She needed the money." Ivy clearly cared deeply for her parents. Her plan for aging in place recapitulated theirs.

Once started on her verbal hike into history, Ivy felt compelled to continue. Older folks often lack people with whom to talk. Today I provided a captive audience. Ivy moved on to her own history: "We needed a larger house as family and bouncy boxer puppy grew. Between the children and the dog, the living room floor was full. Legs and paws everywhere! One couldn't even walk through it! This house [she gestured lovingly to her surroundings] was the perfect solution. Lots of cozy places to spread out, to curl up and read away from the family gaggle. Enough bedrooms for the growing family. Walking distance to school."

"Have you considered long-term care?" I ventured, trying to get to the questions on my interview list. Ivy smiled and told me she planned to die in this house. She had survived the daunting steps—three floors!—when she was pregnant and when she had a broken leg. In the last year or so she cleaned out much of the children's clutter, abandoned as they moved on to build their own lives with fresh stuff. Like her mother she labeled pictures and memorabilia with the names of the original owners—aka the kids—in the hopes that, when she was gone, the house would be orderly, and they could take what was theirs. (Did she not remember complaining about her own saved childhood detritus?)

She confided that wills were in order, including a clear document eschewing any "extraordinary" means to keep her alive. She and Alan had initiated that awkward conversation with the children, so that everyone understood her wishes. The youngest child, who knew her mom so well, was the appointed durable power for health care—just in case Ivy could not defend herself from unwanted heroic interventions.

Files were purged. She burned her diaries in the fireplace one evening, sipping a glass of red wine while they literally went up in smoke. She made a list of the location of important documents and put it in her top desk door with a bright green label on it—just in case the children forgot what she told them. Memory books for each of the children—both their personal memories and those of the family going back four generations—were complete.

"Dear, you must see the basement." (More digression!) That was always the joke she told: I can't die until I clean the basement. (She insisted I see it!) Now its commodious space held some boxes of vintage toys and fading pictures on the walls, early color shots from instant cameras. A metal file stored tax records and a few odds and ends. Everything was labeled. A pile of assorted cardboard boxes spilled out from one corner. Ivy selected from among them when she sent gifts to the grandchildren on birthdays and at the holidays. You never knew what size box was best for this particular item! When she died, she joked, her daughter-in-law could use them to get rid of all the junk.

Yesterday she attended the funeral of a good friend, just a year older than she. It was a quiet and healing affair: some friends, a few relatives, a small urn placed in front of a sparsely decorated church altar. The singing was good, the homily even better. But Ivy felt a deep loss. This woman was about her age. Her BFF group continues to thin out. Now another member was edited out of her dance card—friends available for lingering lunches, where they traded good reads and gently-used jigsaw puzzles. This latest death left a dark pall, still wrapped tightly around Ivy.

When her friend was at home last week recuperating from a bout of pneumonia, she called Ivy, sounding angry. "I started to have trouble breathing again. I went to the hospital, surely dying," she grumbled. "It didn't hurt much. Now I'm mad that I might have to do this all again."

Ivy did not have her friend's co-morbidities: smokers' lung or chronic heart issues. She enjoyed walking and even liked her daily oatmeal, sprinkled liberally with cinnamon and almonds. Did she really want to live into a second century, as had her mother's neighbor? Ivy always said—usually as an addendum to her clean basement comments—that, if she ever ended up in a nursing home drooling into her teacup, they should shoot her. (At least this information answered another required question.)

I admired a photo on the wall, a lighthouse in Maine. Ivy has a cousin there, still in her own home and driving. She told Ivy she planted one hundred geranium plants in her yard. this year. Her cousin is ninety-two. She still climbs in and out of the bathtub by herself and cuts her own toenails. Guess that Maine "pluck and perky" attitude works. The cousin was contemplating trying that new store that promoted juuling—and she even knew what that meant!

From time to time Ivy experiences symptoms like those that pointed to that small lump growing on her breast six years ago. Would the cancer return? Her friend's recent death rekindled her own fears of serious illness.

(Ivy put another log on the fire. The intimacy of the conversation was becoming uncomfortable for me. I shifted awkwardly. I was beginning to feel the need for a bathroom.)

This was not the only friend Ivy lost. Six years ago her college roommate, Patty, died three weeks after being diagnosed with lung cancer. At the time Ivy was dealing with that breast lump. That episode was now a foggy blur, a surreal blip on the timeline of her life. She recovered and went on with life. But as she has grown older, those blips are more frequent: premature beats pounding louder and louder, foreshadowing her own passing. Maybe it was time.

For some reason Ivy needed to chronicle each loss for me. Every detail was stroked and examined. "Then Elaine died." They shared high school choral class, debate, and biology dissection. Ivy loved science; Elaine—not so much. The two friends served as bridesmaids in each other's weddings, birthed children in rapid and parallel sequence. The menu of weekly lunches they shared included an account of the week's activities, tears of real-life pain, giggles of high school memories. They shared so much, lives entwined like tendrils climbing a tree drawing closer each succeeding year. Now there remained few friends left to which Ivy might cling, few friends to accompany her with security and support. She was almost alone. Thank goodness Alan was there. Fifty years of deep friendship and growing love, a sturdy trunk to lean on and love. As the saying goes: "Hug a tree." Her sturdy tree was Alan: Ivy clung closely—literally for dear life!

She told me that at one time her friend lunch group had been a trio. The third member of the group died unexpectedly several years before. Her loss left only a scar, one that twinged rarely. Ivy remembered that, at the last lunch with all three, Julie had ordered peach ice cream for dessert. Julie rarely chose her own dessert. When she was out with her husband, she always bowed to *his* choice of sweet—and he did not like peach ice cream. It consoled Ivy to know that, at least in the end, Julie defined her own person—a least a bit.

Julie wasn't the real spelling of her name. It was Guilia. She immigrated from Italy as an orphan years ago. When she died, a congregation of family and friends gathered to remember this wonderful lady. Except Guilia's husband. He was there, but *his* memory was gone.

Ivy continued to ramble on—that ancient mariner in a turtleneck. I began to see that hers was a life constricted to the point where there were few good friends left, particularly to interact beyond tidbits about the news and weather. Ivy seemed like so many old people who struggle to find rich companions, even someone just to talk to! Today I was that captive audience. It was not the first interview during which I felt trapped. Maybe this was the least I could do, a sort-of "payment" to the volunteers for taking the survey. Maybe Ivy's ramblings *were* giving me the information I sought. Could a nursing home offer what she needed, or would it be a place of even more concentrated loss? After all, nursing homes have a higher percent of people near the age of death than families or neighborhood. (Ivy did share, though, that recently a neighbor of hers was killed by a bus and another died of cancer. I guess even safe neighborhoods attract the grim reaper.)

I shifted my position on the sofa. Ivy again offered me more coffee. I declined. Was there a rest room on the first floor?

When I returned Ivy continued her narrative. It was clear that she really liked to talk about her life, even though the details she proffered went well beyond the rigid boxes of the survey. She figured she had about three more years of physical vigor. Last Christmas she asked her husband, not really jokingly, for a skateboard. He bought her a year's supply of expensive tea instead. She was almost done with the supply. It was very good. Maybe next year she'd get the skateboard. He always surprised her with something she wanted.

Hopefully her mind would last a bit longer than her ebbing energy. She watched a good friend, a brilliant and active woman, become a hollow shell shelved in an Alzheimer's unit of a nursing home with faded linoleum to match its residents' minds. She did not even recognize her husband, the father of her seven children. Her brain seemed a moth-eaten rich fabric. Some elements were still recognizable and beautiful, but the overall pattern was interrupted and destroyed with random holes. Ivy hoped that did not happen to her. She and Alan had talked about it. They both felt the same way.

From what I see, Ivy wants her life to end wrapped up and tidy. She wants to die in her own bed, that "happy death" that everyone imagines. She wants her husband and children to understand how much she loves them. Squabbles at her funeral are not on her bucket list.

Alan may die first, but one never knows. He was so distraught when she had the surgery, even though a little lump is hardly a death sentence. The whole episode hurt him much more than it did her. She had pills for her pain; his was beyond pharmacological power. Nevertheless, it seemed better for him if he died first. If the reverse were to happen, who would tell him where the extra manila folders were? Who would separate the darks from the lights on laundry day—and remember to check pockets for random tissues? Who would console him, when the woman with whom he had spent more than four-fifths of his life was ripped from him? That was too cruel. Ivy was grateful that they had children. If she died first, they would be there.

It is hard to lose deep friendships, to be the one left behind—death by a hundred cuts, bleeding a thousand tears. How hard it is to separate entwined branches without ripping apart both plants! The years resist change, but more actually, loss.

To be the last one standing—or perhaps sitting in a wheelchair because legs have ceased to function—is painful. As I listened to Ivy tell her story, I was glad I was young. I was beginning to understand some of the unavoidable challenges of aging. I guess that's what our professor wanted (in addition to his book!).

Ivy's story made me conclude that an old person in her own home was better off than in a nursing home. Was her energy and acuity a function of her busyness, the fact that her husband was still with her? Was it because she still had this palpable extension of her very self in the home she had created? What I did not yet know was what would happen if she were alone or ill.

I looked at my watch again. It was time. I closed my notebook, stood, said my goodbyes, and prepared to leave. Ivy rose somewhat painfully and came along to the door. She smiled, wished me well. The door closed securely. I sighed and wiped away a small tear.

As I drove back to the main road, the trees hovered silently over me. How many of them would survive another generation of families raising children, mowing lawns, decorating bikes for the yearly block parties? In her full-disclosure narrative Ivy showed me pictures of neighborhood parades, the egg-throwing contests, dressed-up pets and decorated bikes.

Would Ivy still be here in three years, when the study was to be completed with a follow up interview? Would she remember the young woman to whom she opened her door and her life? I did not know the answer. I did not want to think about it!

It's Time

"Now here are your stick and hat, and that,
as you plainly know, is the front door."

(GOODBYE, MR. CHIPS, 1969 MOVIE)

It wasn't that he hadn't thought of retirement: the someday trips he read about in colorful brochures; the leisure to sleep in; no tests to grade, a civilized lunch with friends beyond the noisy faculty cafeteria with its recyclable plastic wear. Last year, at a meeting with his dean, he was asked about his future plans. "Oh, I'll stay on at the university until it stops being fun." They both chuckled.

A full-time university professor for over forty years, he still enjoyed his career. It was his life, his legacy. Never motivated to marry, he had no children. Now that he sat in the endowed chair of Medieval History, installed in a corner two-windowed office, he had more time to think and to write. His colleagues in the department afforded stimulating conversation on topics that few others would appreciate. He enjoyed teaching a graduate course every third semester, a topic of his choosing often leading to an article or an idea for a book. From time to time former students dropped by to chat, detailing their post-college successes. He took pride in believing that his courses contributed at least a modicum of influence on their lives.

Even though he was full professor and had seniority, occasionally he taught the undergraduate introductory course. He did not particularly take to freshmen. Intellectual neophytes, they were just learning to cope with college life. They missed Latin allusions and never got his jokes. Nevertheless, teaching them offered the opportunity to turn on young people to the joys of his field, maybe snag a few majors. He loved to mentor young minds, possibly the future of academe. There was that young Hispanic woman who found the machinations of medieval politics stimulating. She even read a few of the books from the bibliography listed at the end of the syllabus. (Most students never read the online version beyond the required assignments and test dates, or they made paper airplanes from the hard copy!) While she chose a major in business—her parents believed that would guarantee a job—she enjoyed learning about other things. When she frowned at her laptop during class, it was clear she was searching for the answer to a question posed in class and not just checking Facebook.

Surprisingly, the professor loved the football players who populated the evening class. Although much of the time they came to class late and sweaty from practice, they were sincere in their attention. They brought the discipline of their game to the study of history.

Last semester the dean again brought up the question of retirement. When the professor gave his same glib answer, the dean paused for a moment. "Well, Lew, I understand you are still having fun. But it's time. It's time for you to go." He was allowed to finish the term, but by fall someone else would be warming the endowed chair. He should have seen this coming. From time to time the institution purged some of the older faculty: those who cost the university a disproportionate salary; those who had lost their touch with students. It is hard to keep up with contemporary student culture. Time adopts a more rapid pace as one ages.

Fourteen boxes of books. He would miss his commodious office; but truth be told the old building in which it was housed was drafty in the winter, especially in that corner office. But he was prepared, just in case the weather turned. Behind the door there was a geriatric sweater hooked discretely with his cap and gown. Many professors never took their academic garb home; they wore it only once a year. No one paid attention to a patina of dust or deep wrinkles draped on multi-colored professors processing to "Pomp and Circumstance." Proud family lasered only on the nervous graduates.

Last time he moved there were sixteen boxes. Since then some were gifted to students, others loaned to colleagues and not returned, several carried virtuously to the library. The remainder included the original copy of his doctoral dissertation, written on another historian, known for his contribution to Vatican II. The dissertation was published later as a book, available in electronic form for minimal cost, but he still liked to handle the original eight-by-eleven bound copy. He smiled when he remembered the long hours at a typewriter, every change requiring a new sheet of paper. It took more than a year of intense and lonely work to achieve the heady standard set by his mentor, a well-published historian with a masters' degree in English!

Now neatly packaged were the contents of four capacious file drawers and a lockable standing file: old class notes, dog-eared grade books, manila folders with scribbled ideas for articles to read or to write "someday," texts of presentations collected over the years with penciled notes of places to pause. The titles on the folders made him smile. "Oh yes. That convention keynote I gave several years back. It provoked that preening no-nothing Harvard guy to ask a stupid question. I put him in his place with my terse and biting response. Didn't have a clue what he was talking about. He was so angry that he tried to publish a rebuttal argument to my paper. No journal would touch it."

One box was layered with framed diplomas and awards acquired over the years. He held an honorary degree from his undergraduate college. A faux-gold trophy and citation marked that event. He had done a stint for the Higher Learning Commission. They sent him a plaque. Over the years he volunteered for his professional association. He chaired sessions, served on nominating committees, even did a stint as convention planner. At the end of his term they gave him a testimonial and a gift certificate for airfare to his next meeting. The testimonial was professionally framed and hung above his desk. Its glass cover had cracked years ago, when the insecure nail split from the wall. "Should have pounded the bugger in more deeply."

On the credenza there was a picture of his brother's family, a smiling gaggle of Mom, Dad, and the two kids, slightly cloudy in a patina of unredacted dust. The whole office smelled both of academic success and mediocre housekeeping. Those odors were captured now in cardboard, courtesy of the facilities department. The rambling memoir of a forty-year career stared back at him from neat piles of brown boxes. Student helpers were scheduled later in the day to haul the tidy collection to his car. Their deployment was only a short distance away: his recently-rented apartment.

When his retirement was announced, he purged a lot. No need to keep multiple drafts of his updated *vita*. Years ago he stopped chronicling the book reviews and presentations that he still gave occasionally (he was unable to part with the notes, though). The section in his current *vita* read simply: "many reviews and presentations." He tossed old final exams he had kept "just in case there was a question." Their "use by" date expired long ago.

The retirement party held three weeks ago was a wonderful distraction from packing. There were laughs—those teacher stories everyone collects—and a few tears. Retired colleagues returned to campus to "roast" him, albeit lovingly. Current faculty, many he barely knew, stopped in. They probably came only for the food. Attendees clustered together exchanging university gossip and research tidbits between trips to the refreshment table. A former department secretary baked his favorite rum cake. The university food service offered up a spread of predictable munchies: chicken satay, veggies and dip, stuffed mushrooms. And there were shrimp! It was a standing joke that only those of stature got shrimp at their retirement parties.

After the shrimp were gone and lonely crumbs of rum cake circled its desolate plate, a few longtime friends lingered. They talked about how it used to be, when students did not demand A's just for showing up and freshmen already knew how to compose a topic sentence. Gradually, the conversation tray was likewise empty. Goodbyes were coupled to promises. "Call me." "Let's do lunch." "We won't lose touch."

Parties with old friends buoy the spirit. One wants to believe that the cords of connection woven over time will not fray. Nevertheless, some things *will* change. Lunch with the guys in the faculty dining room, the opportunity to gripe about the actions of the always adversarial administration will be unnecessary. Retired faculty can, of course, look forward to the "old fart" luncheons (not how the university bills them), a sop sponsored by the institution from time to time. The food tends toward the unremarkable, but conversation with one's fellow old timers supplies adequate spice.

On his way to the library a couple of weeks ago he ran into that red-headed student, George, the one who came to the university mainly to play football. The professor was not good with names. He could call up where a student sat in class, the topic of her term paper, maybe even some context about family or career plans. Names, on the other hand, were inscribed only in fading grade books. George's name was easy; he came from Georgia—Albany (pronounced by the locals as "Al-*bi*-knee," he was told)—to be exact. George, now a senior, had grown three inches since freshman year. From his confident stride, it was clear he healed from that broken leg, the injury that ended his gridiron career that first year. They chatted briefly, although the professor was hungry for more. He thought it unlikely that he might see the student again. Too bad. He always liked George.

Enough reminiscing! Let the pale past rest. The students were coming in an hour to cart away his stuff. There was time only for a walk around campus before he morphed officially into his new identity: "professor emeritus." Was he like the butterfly, poised to emerge from the protective cocoon spun by a sluggish caterpillar curled for so long in a classroom? Was retirement a new expansive life, when he became more beautiful and could fly?

The university always looked particularly lovely during spring graduation. He paused at his favorite spot, the lilac tree on the north lawn. Today, though, few flowers lingered on its branches. Those that remained looked brown and worn out. Over years he saw the tree grow from the modest bush planted his second year on the faculty. Now it presided over that grassy space, the grand lady whose arms reached higher and higher each year. He always thought it a metaphor for the university goals, and for his own: plant something small and watch it grow into something great. He breathed in what remained of the lilac's perfume, sighed, and moved on.

Was it Wednesday? Yes, that was correct. Hard to remember what day it is, when the structure of classes was over. This was the week between finals and Sunday's graduation. If the weather cooperated, it was held on the expansive quad. The grounds crew made sure everything was transformed: seeded, swept, and trimmed to put on the university's best face. This year's speaker was a seasoned senator from another state. The guy was clearly about to announce a run for president. The captive crowd, graduates, parents, faculty, friends, would listen with limited patience to his platitudes. The college provost always advised the speaker to restrict remarks to fifteen minutes. The senator droned on for thirty.

Today the professor was a lonely figure on the spreading green campus. Few stragglers wandered these paths during this in-between time. Undergrads made the grand exodus last week, departing as soon as their finals were done. Last Friday he watched from his office window as parents struggled to shoehorn large collections of essential college stuff into minivans. Each year the girth of baggage grew, reproducing well in the fertile soil of tiny dorm rooms. Small refrigerators popped up on secondhand-shop tables. Class notes blossomed on built-in desks next to illegal vanilla candles and single-brew coffee makers.

Sometimes clueless parents tried to jam in that extra chair, originally purloined from the cafeteria. This sideshow provided a welcome distraction for the professor. Watching almost kept him from finishing computing grades, due later that day.

And today he too was "due." The dean's words cast their dismal shadow again: "It's time." He must leave. He knew all too well what retirement looked like. Although departing professors talked optimistically of plans to write another book (the one for which they had no time during the busy semester) or to contribute to dialogue in their field, he knew that such plans rarely materialized. He observed the few wizened professors who still attended academic meetings pausing at the fringes of the booksellers' tables, feigning interest in new contributions to their field. One editor called them "lost souls." They tried to appear earnest and professorial, but everyone knew the truth. Mostly they tackled unsuccessfully the *New York Times* crossword puzzle, stared religiously at late night news, and fell into sleep composing that elusive book that existed only in their soporific hopes.

He observed other "mature adults," some conversing earnestly with patient check-out grocery clerks in a lame attempt to bring some social interaction to their world. When he walked around his old neighborhood, he tried to avoid the old lady with the arthritic dog. She always forced an unwanted and prolonged discussion with passersby, much like the ancient mariner of Coleridge's poem. While on vacation in Italy he observed the grim faces of daughters-in-law as they steadied even grimmer *nonnas* on their daily walks. He vowed not to become a burdensome elder citizen.

At family gatherings it was difficult to avoid noticing that his older brother rarely was invited into the conversation—even among his own children. They prattled on about celebrities, of whom he knew nothing. They marveled over the latest smart phone app or discussed how their high school peers could "hook up" on Tinder. The professor thought tinder defined random flammable contributions to a cozy fire on a cold winter night! Few at the table acknowledged his brother's up-to-date computer skills or his passion for opera, a subject he taught for many years at the senior learners' institute. The conversation always floated in an animated bubble well above his geriatric pay grade.

His brother died a few years ago, his bucket list yellowed and neglected. The death was sudden, although his interest in life had diminished slowly during his last years. By the time he passed, he was marginalized not only from his family's life but from his own. The professor was still invited to family get-togethers. He was sure it was on account of duty rather than desire for his company. He rarely attended.

As he ambled through campus—*his* campus for so long—the sun peeked out and dissipated his dark thoughts. His mind wandered again to the past. He recalled his meeting with the well-known academic on whom he wrote his dissertation. He was so excited to interview this icon, by that time retired from his scholarly career and nearing ninety. The tiny home nestled among just-like-me condos at the end of a long-overgrown street. The living room was ornate, fixed in the past: an over-stuffed sofa, uncomfortable chairs with doilies on the headrests, assorted ash trays, and artifacts collected in another time. The house reeked of cigarettes and the dust of many years.

As a beginning scholar, Lew felt uncomfortable in the presence of his idol. As he squirmed nervously and shuffled his notes, he breathed in the smell and the sadness of this discarded man. Although the senior professor answered questions with patience and precision, it was clear that he believed his expertise to be outdated. "Why would anyone care about my work today? If they cared, why do I spend my days alone?" These many years later as he too prepared to become an antique, Lew Johnson, PhD, understood.

Returning to the present, he glanced at his watch. Time for his walk down memory lane to end. He returned to his naked office. To his surprise the students had already removed the stacks of boxes. The computer that delivered so many daily messages from students was gone. A pristine square, surrounded by faded wood, defined the spot it rested for years.

One last look at the empty chair, permanently pleated with the impression of his body, the massive maple desk with the dark stain from spilled coffee, the shelves lined with subtle rows of dust from between the books. These were the dessicated bones of his academic body. As he closed the door for the last time, he noticed the burnished plate: Lewis Johnson, PhD, Chair in Medieval History. He removed it from its holder and carried it with him to the car. Make way for another plate naming his successor.

The sun was near the horizon now, and the delicate breeze of spring had matured into a strong penetrating wind. He cranked up the car's heat and drove deliberately through the parking lot, waving to the guard as he passed the gate. The trip home took barely ten minutes. He eased the car into his heated parking space in the basement of his new apartment building. This was the first time he enjoyed such a luxury.

The books and other stuff could wait. No need to bother today. He likely wouldn't need these things anytime soon. "Maybe never," he thought grimly. A borrowed dolly and several trips on the elevator should do the trick, if he got around to it. Although he chose a two-bedroom space with commodious built-in bookshelves, he was not sure that there was sufficient room to accommodate the contents of all these boxes. Fourteen boxes: his life entombed in somber cardboard, the cremains of his professional career.

The new apartment was cozy. He had been there about two weeks. Between grading exams and packing his office, he managed to create a degree of *kronos* to the *impedimenta* that he brought in. (It was one of his professorial delights to throw pedantic language into his utterances.) A trip to the nearby grocery guaranteed food for the next couple of days, if he wanted anything. His favorite chair was placed just right, the phone installed—he still preferred a landline. Still, none of this gave him comfort.

Professor Johnson decided he was not hungry right now, just exhausted. His chair beckoned. His body ached with the weight of the day. Maybe a pause for the evening cable news? No, not tonight. The day was long and crushing in its sadness. Sterile silence was enough.

Then it occurred to him. Yes, that's what I'll do. He walked briskly into the bathroom. As he had always been for class, for presentations at professional meeting, in all aspects of his life; he was prepared. He grasped the tidy aluminum knob of the medicine cabinet. It was predictably ordered and properly stocked: a toothpaste tube squeezed thin from prudent use, an almost empty bottle of cough medicine from that cold he caught during midterms, a sensible razor—he never liked the electric kind—a newly purchased large-size extra-strength Tylenol. "Yes. There it is." He twisted off the safety seal and opened the bottle. "It's time," he thought. And then the bottle was empty.

A Visit to Sunny Hill

"You are my sunshine. My only sunshine.
You make me happy, when skies are gray."

(AUTHOR DISPUTED)

NURSING HOMES ARE FAMILIAR fixtures in an America of aging baby-
boomers. Glossy mailings and informative websites depict seniors reading to grandchildren, playing tennis, laughing over lunch with friends.
Residents tend gardens, assisted by volunteer horticulturists. Others enjoy
manicured grounds from their windows or from a sheltered porch. One
compelling photo shows a wheelchaired woman embraced by two attendants—one a minority. Others capture a well-groomed octogenarian, fork
poised to tame a steak, or a wrinkled hand patting the head of a Welsh
terrier. The slightest suggestion of interest provokes a call from marketers.
Friends tell me how well Mom or Dad, Aunt Sally or Uncle Josh are doing
in their respective nursing homes.

As a "senior citizen" myself, I have some personal curiosity. I pour
over a brochure for Sunny Hill, grabbed from a rack when I happened to
be there a few weeks ago. The glossy three-fold encourages older adults to
deposit the remainder of their lives with them—a secure investment with
dividends. For those not up to cooking carrots or to chasing tennis balls,
the leaflet promises meals and activities designed for "independent" living
or "long-term care." Visits to cultural events and museums are provided—
no need to scrape snow from chilly cars. The van with wheelchair access is
"free."

In their literature many homes suggest tours (lunch and speaker included) to introduce potential clients to their facilities. Satiated attendees

get the hard-sell pitch, which paints a bucolic landscape of care. The reality is not so always so "independent," and "long term" is often code for "I will inhale only stuffy institutional air until my last breath."

No photographs document the vacant look of demented or bedridden residents. None suggest feeding tubes or atrophied lives. None show the grim faces of the emergency squad workers, resolutely fetching the skin-and-bones body of a recent nursing home dropout. All promotional materials use adjectives like "nurturing, active lifestyle, and home-like" to sell their product.

Today my husband and I are on our way to Sunny Hill to visit a long-time friend, Manny. We drive slowly past a park, a neighborhood soccer field, residential streets lined with mature trees. We see a young mother walking her baby, bundled against the wind. We turn into the parking lot. Its asphalt expanse is generous enough to accommodate reluctant relatives as well as loyal friends. Special places are designated for "Doctors" and "Visitors." Hard choice: my husband is both. We ease into a close-in spot. Not many visitors today, unlike Sunday when large groups of volunteer students swarm in to wheel patients who cannot walk to the uninspiring Catholic Mass that punctuates the quotidian monotony of the residents.

One of my high school students confided in me how she cried the first time she volunteered here. Connie was excited about her senior service project. The reality dampened her enthusiasm. She had never seen so many old people in one place, many unable to walk, warehoused, as they wait for death. It was an image she could not shake. It broke her heart. As she told me about her experience after class last week, tears formed again.

The rotating Sunday priest always hurries through the ritual, anxious to be released from the terminal congregation he serves. The *double entendre*, "Go in peace," suggests permission to die. Sporadically local churches send well-meaning but poorly trained lay ministers to bring communion. Congregations from different denominations provide prayer leaflets and pious words to punctuate the routine of daily living. The order of nuns that used to staff the facility had too few sisters to continue their ministry here. St. Jude's Home morphed into Sunny Hill. I guess the evolution from an institution named for the saint of hopeless causes to a place of verdant growth is good. Today is Saturday. No service is on the schedule.

Just a few years ago Manny was a vital person. He was persistently interested in people, in trying new things, and in the life of his Catholic parish. Tall and a natty dresser, he was spotted easily at the center of any group. His laugh bubbled up from a barrel chest, identifiable in a theater audience whenever an actor delivered a funny line. If a friend looked depressed, Manny probed until he discovered the source of pain. He provided whatever salve would ease hurt. His piano playing was old standards, sometimes by ear and sometimes with assistance of dog-eared binders of sheet music. It was the glue that held any party together. A picture on his window sill shows him at the piano, fixed in time as he laughs with friends. They sing hit standards from a former era: "You Can't Take That Away from Me," "You Are My Sunshine," "Always." Oh, Manny, you are my sunshine—always. Or you used to be.

When a new play or restaurant came to town, Manny was the first to drag along his friends to check them out. For many years he served as a lector in his church. His rich tenor animated the scriptural word better than most. Even in his eighties, he drove to work each weekday. No sick days stained his record. Although his duties lightened in recent years, he kept his arthritic hands and mind in the hardware business, assisting in any way possible.

Nor was he ready to pack in his love life. A widower, he searched online until the perfect girlfriend caught his eye. Marge rivaled him in education and fit comfortably into the void left by the death of Manny's wife, Julie. Since they both still worked, the new couple had only weekends to spend together—at her home or his. Marriage proved to be too complicated a choice.

When they became a couple we reinstated our weekly Saturday lunch, a fixture of our long relationship with Manny and Julie. For a while we sampled new restaurants, often adding a red wine to elevate the meal; but as Manny's driving skills diminished to the point of producing terror for his passengers, we stayed closer to home. Now Sunny Hill is his home and lingering lunches are no more.

Manny has been there for several months. That is how long it takes the average resident to adjust to this new way of living. A fall—apparently one of a series that he had neglected to mention to his family—precipitated a visit to the primary care doctor. The physician tested Manny for both physical and mental acuity. His patient should no longer drive or live alone in the home where his abundant family had grown up and grown away.

Grudgingly Manny set up housekeeping on the pull-out couch in his son's family room. It was a comfortable space, set off from the rest of the house for privacy; but the first-floor half-bath did not allow the luxury of a shower or tub. Although there were three bedrooms upstairs, his legs could not brave the stairs. In close quarters, family stress grew. He and his divorced son, Jerry, argued frequently. Jerry encouraged his dad to try, to exercise more, to take an interest in his well-being. Manny resisted the well-meaning urgings. Mostly he just watched television.

While Jerry was at work, Manny increasingly spent weekdays in a day-care facility. For the pick-up van to take him, he was required to walk to the end of the driveway. At least that gave his reluctant body a modicum of movement. The outings offered opportunities to make new friends, but the circle of the life he inhabited grew increasingly smaller.

Repeated respiratory infections earned him a series of hospital stays, rehab, and the permanent label of "old." While these admissions brought him attention as well as additional therapy, they did not motivate him to get better or to re-engage life.

Finally, some other arrangement was indicated. His other two children lived out of town. Jerry and the married daughter who lived in town had woven their lives into secure webs that did not accommodate an additional person, particularly one who needed considerable assistance in every aspect of daily life. It was time. He must go to the nursing home. There was no viable alternative. When the decision was made, Manny uncharacteristically said little. He merely shrugged.

Before settling on Sunny Hill, he and his son considered other places. They went on the tours to allow him to choose the one he liked best. None worked out. One popular home turned down his application; others were priced beyond his modest savings. Sunny Hill was the last resort. And its reputation was good.

My husband and I visit regularly. Most of the time we come together, sharing the heavy package of guilt and reluctance that we always bring. Saturdays are the most convenient. Today is Saturday. As usual, we take a deep breath and head for the main entrance. It's time.

Just outside the automatic glass doors we pass a resident in her wheelchair. She shelters under the entrance canopy, a red plaid blanket tucked around her wasted legs. She is enjoying a change of scene and an animated conversation with her daughter. A squirming toddler, along to visit Grandma, concentrates on a curious squirrel.

A tired employee on a cigarette break stands nearby, leaning against the brick wall. Fortunately the smoke is blowing in the opposite direction. We push the shiny square that magically opens the door.

The generous woman at the sign-in desk smiles as we arrive. She knew my husband from his tenure as medical director here; we are greeted warmly. Still, we are required to offer up our names and time of arrival on lined pages captured on a clipboard. Flimsy badges identify us as acceptable visitors. Such precautions protect the residents and the facility from unwanted guests.

Each time the familiar formula repeats. Sign in. Walk briskly through the public area, down the hall to the *sostenuto* elevator. Push the button to the fourth floor. Get out of the elevator. Breathe deeply as we navigate the dreary corridor to prepare for the difficult visit. Smile at other residents: those with severe physical challenges, the limping lady who helps out in the library, the grandma who knits a warm shawl of connection to a little girl on the common computer, the man with the vacant stare. Visit briefly. Say our goodbyes. Leave.

The home provides additional security for memory-impaired residents, as some tend to wander. They live in a protected pocket, a locked unit ironically named, Little Lea—small meadow. There is not any real meadow—large or small—beyond its secure doors. Having deposited their loved ones there, families can relax, feeling good about their decision. Manny does not live in the "meadow."

No flimsy name tag or key keeps residents in any part of the home from underpaid night workers who steal pocket money and incidentals from sleeping charges. Families know about this, but nothing much can be done. Perhaps the old folks merely forget where they put their new shirt, their watch, their wallet. Perhaps the underpaid workers believe they deserve additional compensation for the difficult work they do.

As usual today we continue through the facility's public area. Pale walls and wooden beams flank an inviting fireplace. It is cold enough to warrant a crackling blaze. Clusters of soft chairs upholstered in bright green and beige plaid offer families and their loved ones an alternative to visiting in the claustrophobic bedrooms that line the empty halls. In the common space visitors can avoid the sight of patients who sit despondently in their wheelchairs, heads bowed, waiting for the family that never comes.

Trees trapped forever indoors add texture to the area. A vending machine features fast foods in sterile plastic. Tired bags of chips and candy bars enjoy no privacy from human eyes choosing their cholesterol fix. An enclosed aviary allows tropical birds a place to live, if not a horizon toward which to fly free. It appears that the birds are singing. We discover that someone sitting in the lounge has found a bird noises app on his cell phone. Electronics give ersatz voice to the silent prisoners perched, defeated, behind the glass.

A family group sits in the main lobby. The patient's plastered leg and his lively demeanor suggest he is a temporary resident, probably here only for rehab. Someone nearby has brought in what appears to be a therapy dog—a black bear of an animal with a look of boredom. He tugs slightly on his lead as the family chats quickly.

We pass the tiny gift shop. Earnest volunteers display their inventory of artificial plants, small stuffed animals, and a few other items for residents or guilty visitors who wish to pick up a last-minute offering. Others offer their time to provide books or supervise activities that punctuate the routine. Off to the side in the "party room" a young pianist accompanies thready voices on an out-of-tune upright. The room is spacious enough for a bevy of folding chairs. It can be reconfigured to host small family events, volunteer concerts, or a somber memorial service. A large crucifix hovers on the north wall, over a raised podium. Likely it is a leftover from the days when the home was run by Catholic nuns, or perhaps from the Sunday service. A box of tissues sits thoughtfully on the window sill. Today the space is empty.

Last week the parking lot was unusually full for a Saturday. As we left, we found out why. One of the resident's families booked the room to mark their mother's birthday. The word *celebrate* did not seem to fit. The modest group clustered in the small carpeted section near the windows. Perhaps this area was designed for such affairs, as the faded carpet appears to define a space for a limited gathering. No one brought musical life to the failing piano. The carryout food, meatball sandwiches, looked cold.

The diminishing birthday girl sat alone in her wheelchair, waiting without emotion for the party to begin. She was the inanimate "sacred object," like the turkey at Thanksgiving dinner. Rituals need a focus, a requisite site prop, the iconic oak where offerings to the gods were laid by reluctant attendees.

Today we wonder if Manny will be interested in conversation. We might tell him about that birthday party. We'll tell him about the large meatballs. Manny likes meatballs. We won't tell him they were cold.

The elevator is slow of course, but we are not in a hurry. Perhaps the doors' inertia is a calculated mechanism, a pause long enough to allow self-propelling older people in wheelchairs the time to enter without being crushed by impatient doors. Push the "Close door" button a couple of times. Create the illusion of control.

We make our way down the hall to Manny's floor. Forgettable pictures of spring flowers framed in faux wood break the monotone of mint-green walls. A lone walnut china cupboard cloisters a collection of Royal Doulton figures, a legacy ceded by a former resident. Probably both the relatives and the resale shop rejected them. Another antique is a tired picture of the dying Jesus, hanging crooked on the wall next to the breakfront. No market for beloved possessions of the dead or departed nuns. At a small computer room on our left, a grandmother enjoys electronic face time with a young child. Both sound enthusiastic. Farther down the corridor a thumb-tacked notice indicates the hours of the beauty shop and a list of the week's activities. At the end of the hall an alcove sits empty. Under the former management, it housed a plaster statue of the Virgin Mary. Like many previous residents, Jesus' mother is gone.

Manny's room is near the end. An intrusive noise marks our steps. Buzz. Buzz. Buzz. Buzz. Someone either has called for help or gotten up from a wheelchair. Many older people are unsteady on their feet. Life spent primarily in a wheelchair erodes both strength and balance. Nursing homes install buzzers on wheelchairs to minimize falls and broken bones. They alert staff to unauthorized resident movement. Falls count as violations when the regulating agency comes to certify the nursing home. So does resident weight loss, which dictates high-nutrition liquid supplements to prevent dwindling. If a resident has difficulty swallowing, or if ingested fluids find their way into the airway to the lungs rather than where they belong, thickening agents may be added to everything liquid in their diets. These agents alter both the taste and consistency, but they help to prevent lung infections.

Today no one is responding to the incessant call. Buzz. Buzz. Neither institutional carpeting nor gracious antiques buffer the noise that interrupts the dead-end atmosphere that dominates this place. From a room down the hall someone is pleading, "Nurse, nurse." No one responds. Overworked staff become inured to those whose desperate pleas signal no real need. Parsimonious pay translates easily into indifference.

For a moment we move to the side to allow a gurney to pass. They are transferring someone to the hospital. Declining elderly people often require hospitalization. The urinary tract, particularly in a sedentary or incontinent person, offers a perfect haven for bacteria. Pneumonia, another complication for nursing home patients, guarantees a weekend pass to the hospital for assessment and aggressive antibiotic treatment. Modern drugs often prolong the "long" in long-term care. They cure infections that used to be deadly. Pneumonia, for example, was called the old person's "friend." A generation ago, deaths from pneumonia were not uncommon; nursing homes were.

We are early today, well before the "festive, nutritious, and tasty" lunch. As we walk quickly by the sterile dining area—McDonald's efficiency without the arches—workers place spoons and paper place mats on barren plastic tabletops. The staff look tired. It is the end of a long shift. One man looks up from his task and smiles. I am distracted for a moment, wondering whether diners are allowed the use of real forks and knives or if they must tackle their meals with plastic. It probably does not matter. The food is over-cooked and soft.

There is little to encourage visitors to linger in this sterile space. Like the food, it is devoid of color. Chairs are sparse. Wheelchairs transport most of the residents, just as soon as staff has time to push them. Sometimes staff walk their charges to meals, but that requires additional minutes and attention—and probably a motivating order written in the chart.

Manny's room resembles a neglected creamed coffee, cold and unappetizing—a sepia snapshot of the promise it held when the facility was built thirty years ago. Privacy is compromised by the door perennially open to the hall and to the bath shared with the neighboring room. Its wide door gapes open, exposing the intimate facilities within. The bedroom furnishings are minimalist and functional: a hospital bed noticeably rumpled, a narrow bureau for clothes, a small steel desk equipped with a landline, a box of tissues, and a neglected book. Laundry from the last change of bed linen lies in disarray on a chair, two freshly-cased pillows prop precariously on top, a cheap plastic hanger sequesters beneath. On the postage-stamp bedside table a box of picked-over candies competes for space with a carry-out container of broken cookies, a device to improve breathing, and a pen. The stale smell of neglect emanates from the puny pile.

A paltry collection of books and some family photos snuggle on the window sill. The pictures document large, laughter-filled gatherings: dad with daughters; dad with sons, husband and wife. Happier times; closer relationships. The books are the same ones we saw there a month ago. When he first came to Sunny Hill, Manny devoured their library collection. Now he reads little.

The window frames a pastoral scene anchored by a neglected garage. Stunted weeds strain from its driveway. Beyond the concrete, crocuses push up optimistically against the wind. Purple, yellow, and white, they play freely on rolling hills that comprise the nursing home property, hills not designed for rolling chairs.

A geriatric television carries on a one-way conversation with its dozing owner. Was this device the legacy of a former resident who has passed? Was it spared the hell of Goodwill to reside in the purgatory of Sunny Hill? For an additional fee, the brochure notes, the nursing home can provide a modern set. We move the bed linen from the chair and sit down.

At Sunny Hill routine orders get Manny a daily dose of physical therapy. The young physical therapy aide, Max, brings animation to the room. Each day before lunch, he bounds in, positive energy and joy oozing from every pore. From around his waist he undoes the bands designed to help lift his patient from the wheelchair. The regime: a single short walk down the hall, a brief routine of stretching four limbs for several minutes each. Then duty calls the therapist to the next patient.

Even though the therapy aide has requested it more frequently, the facility does not provide therapy at other times. Manny exhibits no will to work out on his own. Watching him resist even the gentle advice to move his legs is frustrating. He seems to shrivel more deeply into his own skin. Some label him "stubborn." Others think him "lazy." He is impassive to most everything from the constant hall noise and bland meals to any goal that yearns for more. The pen on the bedside table is idle; there is no bucket list. Perhaps Manny has decided he is done with life, anchored as he is to the wheelchair. Its buzzer is silent. Depends can take care of any accident.

Written orders provide him with "assistance" to eat—those thickeners to help him swallow liquids. Family members want to prevent pneumonia. Another bout might kill him. The nursing home agrees. Thickeners do not increase his appetite, as they worsen the taste of the already unimaginative food.

Written instructions—however rigid and complete—apparently do not require anyone to check to see if Manny's oxygen is working properly, as it appeared to be turned to "off" when we were last there. That day Manny appeared worse than usual. Diminished and fragile, we found him fast asleep in the wheelchair, the oxygen cannula intended to help his breathing competing with a small drip at the tip of his nose. Predictably, the television was on, ignored by the person who no longer connects with life, who has let go of interest in much of anything. As we entered, he gradually awoke.

Manny used to enjoy the weekly bingo games. They serve wine. Wine is less festive when its consistency mimics pudding. He stopped going to bingo. His appetite is clearly in retreat. That partially eaten box of candy sits untouched on the window sill. It has been there for a month. Maybe an order for Ensure is coming soon. Residents' weight must be maintained.

After he is awake, we try to make conversation, mostly rattling off profound inanities to fill the awkward gaps. I prattle on about things of no interest even to me. We ask questions hoping for content-rich replies. Manny responds with short answers. "No, we weren't able to go out to the museum. Yes, cousin Mike came to visit last week. Hmm. No, I don't know what that out-of-town grandchild is doing these days." It is hard to tell whether the truncated conversation is the fault of failing ears or failing memories. Perhaps it is a manifestation of depression, certainly understandable. In any case, the conversation resembles that of an awkward first date: lots of pauses and ahs, very little content, unease all around. Manny does not seem to notice.

I notice. I am angry, frustrated. I want to scream, wave a magic wand, make this all go away. A problem solver, I urge Manny to set a goal of ten minutes a day of leg lifting, reading, some commitment to make things better. How can anyone not care? Manny, there *are* things you *can* do! Isn't there anything you *want* to do?

It is hard for me to allow his circumstances just to *be*, so I am always happy for any excuse to avoid what has become an increasingly painful hour each week. Each time when we do come my husband and I exchange the bundling up against the parking lot wind for bundling up emotions that mask concern. Maybe I want to remain bundled up also against the frustration of Manny!

Manny's name in a plastic holder on his door verifies the presence of the person we used to know. There is no picture to show others who he used to be. "Hello, old guy. How're ya doing?" The upbeat greeting does not yield a response in kind.

My husband, who cares deeply, wracks his brain to think about ways to stimulate Manny to take an interest in life. Although not one to share his feelings, he too seems frustrated by Manny's intransigence. His latest idea was to suggest that Manny think about what he can do for others at Sunny Hill. Maybe that will be the electric spark that shocks him back to his old self.

How do vital persons become the equivalent of neglected house plants? I grieve for the Manny departed. I grieve for the gift he was as friend, informal confessor with generous absolution, a goad to be more involved in life than I would have chosen on my own. A veritable Zorba, he used to dance and laugh and lavish his friends with attention and love. Now he was a plain vanilla person, a cipher in an unremarkable list of numbers, a life signed only in shallow breathing and shallower conversation.

Modern medicine creates expensive pills to banish toenail fungus or saggy neck skin, or to conquer runaway heart beats. Trips to the bathroom can be magically minimized or prudently increased—depending on the condition. Physical and even psychic pain is brought to its knees by expert titrations of pharmaceutical wizardry. Skilled technicians salvage our failing organs and refit our bodies with expertly constructed pieces and parts. Why is there no chemistry to repair the person? What replenishes the joy and purpose that makes life *life* and not mere survival? Where is the lost and found center to reinstall in our missing friend?

My heart aches for a return to the grand parties we had, the memory of the many family weddings where he provided the music—even more the love. We continue to visit this faded man in his faded room. But my heart grieves that Manny doesn't live there anymore, no matter what the name tag on the door says.

Originally, I wrote this piece to dampen my own sadness. My husband believes I wrote it to dissipate the anger I felt at a situation that I could not change. When I wrote it, I feared that Manny would die soon. He looked so frail, so "done" with living. Maybe I just wished that were the case. Since it appeared that his memory was fading, death would be relief. Our weekly visits to the nursing home would be over. The heavy chit of guilt could be redeemed for grief, an emotion that would pass.

Sometimes it appears things are looking up. Manny, always the ladies' man, finds a new friend and with that a sliver of new life. Marge, the friend he had met online, is still in touch: but she no longer drives. Enter Sarah: an attractive and energetic volunteer. She decides to start a group for residents who love opera. Manny is delighted. He begins to take interest in the weekly opera sessions, listening with fellow residents to the rich music he loves—even without a glass of wine. He begins to take interest in Sarah as well as others in the group. It occurs to me that I might retitle the piece: "Manny Finds Hope."

Sadly, that title will not work. Even the intense joy of listening to opera each week barely merits discussion or enthusiasm. He does not always remember which opera they reviewed.

Has he made peace with the fact of his permanent confinement in a cubicle? While it is not quite a proper coffin, it is the next-to-last stop on the way. He appears to accept the constant noise in the hall: the buzzer unanswered, a faraway phone with a persistent ring, the moans of lonely old ladies. He cares nothing for what's on the next month's menu or the stimulating activities listed on Sunny Hill's brochure (glossy pictures included). My question lingers. Has he made peace with this reality, or does he no longer care?

Mostly he has let go of his own history. He rarely mentions the past, his happy days in college, the friends who were so close to him. The plays he has seen, the books he has read, the parade of experiences from a rich life are all packed away in dusty trunks stored in an attic to which he has lost the key. Or perhaps he knows where it is and doesn't really care.

Centuries of Catholic piety called believers to be indifferent to creatures and all created happiness, to accept whatever God sends, to offer God the pain of life's reality. After that, they may accept with gratitude the carrot at the end of the Christian stick: eternal happiness with God in heaven. "Don't worry, be happy." Sadly, I cannot buy that narrative. I want to write a different tale.

Today is Saturday. It's time. It's time for our visit Sunny Hill. The weather forecast is bleak: cloud cover and freezing rain.

Sex in Green Garden

"The man and his wife were both naked, yet they felt no shame."

(GENESIS 3)

ELMER AND EVE MARRIED more than fifty years ago. She was a dental hygienist, he a salesman. That's how they met. She knew he had good teeth, and that it was difficult for him to keep his mouth shut.

A faded wedding picture sits on the mantle: bride and groom in fifties formal, crusted in gold. It is flanked by photos of Scottish terriers—four, to be exact—that were loved from puppyhood to death. There are no children, but their sex life was active. They joked that they had sex in twenty different countries but brought home no "souvenirs." They liked to take a week or two off and go someplace fun. After retirement they traveled even more. They sampled sushi in Tokyo and prosecco along the Arno in Florence. They laughed together, grieved their lack of offspring, and moved on. And then things changed.

Now in his late seventies, Elmer has dementia. Eve began to notice his memory loss two years ago, when he could not find his way back to that tiny bed and breakfast in Paris. Creatures of habit, they had stayed there two or three times over the years. It was convenient and welcoming. Each time they requested the same room—no surprises even though it was not a Holiday Inn! They knew the names of the staff and even lunched with the manager. They loved to return to many of the same restaurants, avoiding tourist traps and predictable attractions. They did homage to the *Mona Lisa* almost every time they came, but more recently they concentrated on hidden gems that did not draw the crowds.

Even in foreign cities Elmer never asked for directions, though he loved to schmooze and knew enough words to do so in most countries: "*Dove? Ou? Wo?*" A keen sense of direction always got him to where he wanted to go, so he never carried a map. And he knew Paris very well!

Perhaps he just got distracted that day. He went out for a bottle of wine (they enjoyed a drink before bedtime; sex to follow) and did not return for over two hours. Eve chalked it up to a long discussion with the shop owner, or at least that was what Elmer told her when he finally showed up. The rest of the stay was uneventful, and the wine and its aftermath were wonderful!

From time to time he forgot the name of a friend, but his wife assured herself that all of us do that. One day he put away the ice cream in the cupboard where the cereal was kept. The mess wasn't too bad, but Eve resolved to check after him whenever he helped her put away groceries. And then she posted discreet signs on the cabinet doors. He must have too much on his mind. Yes, that's it. He's distracted. After all, she was facing a possible knee replacement. She was in increasing pain, especially on the stairs. They both knew she needed surgery. Eve knew his concern for her was always greater than her own.

As time went on the reality could no longer be denied. Like Eve's knee pain, things were getting worse. One Tuesday Elmer took the grocery list from the kitchen bulletin board. He gave Eve a peck on the cheek, smiled and left for the store. It was nine in the morning. Elmer did not return until the police brought him home at dark—without the milk carefully underlined on the list! Eve was relieved and devastated at the same time. She spent the day frantically calling friends, imagining a serious auto accident, even wondered—without reason—if he had simply left her. Was there a suitcase sequestered in the car? Was that kiss a permanent goodbye?

With her pain growing worse and surgery imminent, Elmer was going to need a more monitored care than she was able to give. The assistance of a devoted wife was not enough, no matter how many signs she placed on cupboards and how many times she called his cell while he was away. It was time for Elmer to move to Green Garden. The facility provided ongoing care not only for healthy residents but also for people with dementia. Eve talked with friends and their primary care doctor. She was referred to a neuropsychologist, who recommended the facility highly. It was close to their home, just around the corner. Before Eve's orthopedic issues she and Elmer liked to walk around the grounds and admire the flowers. Depending on the time of day the residents who planted them could be seen watering or weeding their prized roses. The sprawling property boasted winding walkways and many mature trees. From time to time Elmer talked about volunteering there—it was so beautiful—but their frequent travel made that impossible.

They visited a good friend who lived there for several years before he died. The capacious halls boasted beautiful antiques, a history gifted by residents both current and deceased. The efficient staff fussed over the furniture with the same care they offered to the residents. Green Garden always got A ratings from nursing home inspectors. It was one of the few places Eve previewed that did not smell! She felt good about her choice.

Now it was a year later. Elmer was admitted to the facility. As predicted, it took him almost six months to settle in. Eve has recovered from her surgery and taken down the labels from the cupboards. Now that she can walk without terrible pain, she goes every day. Usually she brings a treat: his favorite chocolate cookies from the neighborhood bakery, a small bottle of lemoncello tucked under her coat or some wine in a hot-beverage container (the facility is a sober only place), sometimes a croissant to remind him of Paris.

She sighs as she walks into his room. It is cheery. The sun pours in and lights up the space. On the shelf is their wedding picture, ceded from the mantle at home. Eve brought the picture in to remind him of their relationship. Draped on the bed is a splashed-with-color woolen throw bought on one of their trips to Spain.

Eve smiles as she remembers that same throw wrapped around her naked body in a small Barcelona bedroom. She was munching on an apple. She took a waist-up picture of Elmer with the same throw draped across his shoulders. He is holding a glass of tequila, jaunty lime perched on its rim. They had such fun together in those days. Eve remembers. Elmer does not.

Elmer's private space is chock full of lovely things, reminders of happier days; Elmer's eyes are empty, memories chewed away by his disease. A sliver of recognition seems to cross his face as his wife comes in. Then it fades. He greets her with, "Where is Eve? She never comes to visit me." The staff tells her that he poses the same sad question to them, again and again several times a day. The question is as painful to her as it appears to be to Elmer.

Often Eve stays for lunch, reminding her husband of his favorite foods and sometimes leaning over to wipe a stray piece of salad from his chin. The touch is tender; she loves him deeply. After lunch she escorts him gently back to the secure area that protects residents with memory impairment from wandering. She reminds him that there is singing around the piano on the activity schedule for tonight. Remarkably, one of the residents with dementia still plays by ear. Elmer loves to sing. His rich basso dominates the group. Many of the residents' voices have thinned out along with their ability to remember. Some cannot recall the words and just hum along.

Elmer is able to dress himself, even if sometimes his socks don't match or he puts his shirt on inside-out. To the average observer he appears normal—for an old guy, they might add. When he's with his buddies he loves to talk in detail about his trips with Eve. It is one of the few things he remembers. As he tells his tales he occasionally even suggests the suggestive—and laughs at his good joke. If she could hear his stories, Eve would blush.

Elmer still navigates the long hall from his room to the common bathroom. (Green Garden is a gracious old retirement home. It has no private baths.) That's where he met Lilith. She smiled at him one day as he traveled urgently to his comfort station. Since then, he takes to the hall more frequently, sometimes only to get a glimpse of that girlish smile.

The nursing home encourages friendships among residents. Elmer and Lilith like that. Social interaction helps slow the decline of a fading mind. Many residents, even a few in the memory-impaired unit, remain active physically, enjoying excursions in the handicapped-accessible bus clearly labeled *Green Garden* on its pristine pickle-hued sides. The facility provides opportunities for travel to cultural events, lovely small-group lunchrooms on each floor, services for residents that include everything from hairdressers to ice cream vendors. Lilith especially enjoys the ice cream socials with Elmer.

For many years Lilith taught school. She never married. Her family consisted of phalanx after phalanx of fourth graders who passed through her bright and challenging classroom. She loved teaching, but the ebbing of energy that it required finally pushed her into retirement. Since there were no relatives, she consigned her furniture and her destiny to Green Garden. It was a secure place both for a retired life as well as more care as needed in later years. After a few years, her memory, too, lost some of its "energy." The staff helped her move her things into the memory-impaired unit. Then she met Elmer. His companionship added a brightness to her day, a warm light she managed to remember.

From about 7:30 to 9:00 in the evening, allowing some time after the communal dinner for a walk around the fenced grounds directly off the unit or evening news on the television in the formal living room, residents are assisted with bathing and settled in for the night. For most, this ritual is followed by a bit more television, a chapter in a book checked out of the facility library, or an early bedtime. For some, there is only a vacuum. They simply go to sleep.

One dusky winter evening an aide pops randomly into Lilith's tidy room. She finds Lilith and Elmer engaged in something quite different from late night news. They have discovered a more lively diversion. Each holds a paper cup, which they try to hide when the aide walks in. The cups hold the hidden hooch Eve smuggled in the day before. The couple are nestled sheepishly on the narrow bed.

Sexual activity was not something expected between folks of retirement home age, particularly between a married man and an unmarried woman in a nursing home. While one might overlook such fraternization among unmarried competent residents—consenting adults—this is something different. Apparently this "arrangement" has been going on for a few months. And, from what the aide observes, the relationship is convincingly "consenting." Of course neither of the participants mentioned it to staff or other residents. Nor had Eve heard the news.

Once she has left for the day Elmer's mind omits the small detail of his marriage. Does that make this situation less troubling, or moreso? Lilith, even if not fully competent, has the freedom to form intimate liaisons—or does she?

The staff member is, to say the least, troubled by what she witnessed. She tells her supervisor, who is equally upset. The home originally was started by a strict Methodist group. Its moral tenets forbid marital sexual relations among people not married to each other, particularly if one of the parties has a spouse lurking in the wings. But this is a private matter between two consenting adults. Or is it?

The moral questions are abundant, not to mention the titillating nature of the news. Everyone has an opinion. Buzzing conversations among the staff multiply like mosquitoes, never mind HIPAA rules about patient privacy. Eve is called in for a "meeting." The sober faces of the administrator and his assistant frighten her. Was Elmer dying? Lost? The meeting was brief. Eve must take Elmer home from time to time for some intimate visits.

Eve is not so sure. She thinks about calling a lawyer. The home certainly must be liable. Before the lawsuit can be resolved, Elmer dies. But he dies happy.

House Call

"Good night, sweetheart, till we meet tomorrow."

(RAY NOBLE, 1931)

AT NINETY-FIVE, MY MOTHER is not the woman who dried my tears and taught me how to make filo dough filled with fresh apples and butter and thinly chopped walnuts. She no longer sits on my bed to sing me to sleep with the soothing words of "Good Night, Sweetheart." I wipe my tears silently and out of her sight. It is difficult to watch her diminish.

First the doctor told her she should not drive anymore. For awhile a neighbor took her to the store whenever she needed something, but the lack of mobility made that too difficult. Now I shop for her once a week, mostly easy-heat meals; but she needs more care. My sister and I come almost every day. After she wakes, has her bath, and gets dressed—ever so slowly—we arrange her gently in her favorite chair. She bought this lovely wingback on a meager budget during the first years of her marriage. It was during the depression and good furniture was cheap. A new afghan, a birthday gift from her youngest granddaughter, covers its wearing and faded fabric.

Marie, now a well-respected doctor, made the afghan herself. On its quilted surface are embroidered rainbows and colorful flowers. Grandma used to watch Marie, probably about nine at the time, draw bright and happy pictures: gardens of warmth and bright color. Grandma loved to be with the little ones then. Many years later when she put together memory books for each grandchild, the pictures were pasted lovingly into bulging pages. They were given as Christmas gifts in the year they each turned eighteen. Marie's was full of flowers and rainbows.

Mom doesn't scrapbook anymore. Neither does she eat much these days. Teeth are missing. Soft food is all she can manage. She loves the scones from the bakery near us, but even these require lubrication in her cream-infested tea before she can eat them. She prefers the cranberry ones. They don't have hard-to-chew nuts.

Faded and weak, today she has a bout of indigestion. She retches with discomfort, even after the food is gone. We watch, impotent, and grieve her pain. Although we love her deeply, there is little we can do. The symptoms get worse. We should not wait any longer. It's time. We call her doctor, a longtime family friend.

Perhaps this is the end. She has been in a wheelchair for several years. Her legs, too tired to support her any longer, finally turned in their letter of resignation. Her hearing is impaired and getting worse. Her eyes have, as they say, "seen better days." While her spirits are generally good, some days tears come to cleanse away the pain of friends and family lost. Sometimes they come in abundance. She has survived the loss of her husband and the precipitous death of her baby sister, when she was just the age of her youngest grandson now. Every day we read the obituaries to her. Last year her college roommate, always a confidant, died. Almost every friend from her long life is gone. It seems more than a single person can bear.

The bell at the back door rings. The doctor comes quietly into the room. His dress is casual, a pair of comfy cords and a rumpled sweater under a short windbreaker. His cell announced our call as he was on his way home from his granddaughter's basketball game. He never leaves home without his phone. It's a lifeline, in every sense of the word, to his patients. He is no TV medic, posturing through the screen with a stroked chin and slight frown.

Today he bears no identifying doctor badge, no stethoscope or little black bag—that appendage today only a cliche. He wears no professional armor: the white coat to define him or to defend him from the pain he, too, feels. Family stand by quietly. They know this man, his expertise not in need of "show." He has practiced compassion and competence over many years and many patients. While the bells and whistles of modern medicine are helpful to him, technology and tests generally are used only to confirm his astute conclusions.

He greets the failing woman by name. "Hello, Mrs. D. How are you feeling? I understand it's been a tough day for you." He takes her hand gently, sensing the pulse and assessing the coldness of the fingers. Has the tired heart begun to falter? Sometimes that symptom signals the coming of the end. Like a losing army banding together for its last stand, the body clusters its warmth into a tighter and tighter place as it awaits the tragic end of the final battle. Hands and feet cool, grow cold, and finally stop their movement.

He places hands gently on her chest. Hmm. No sign of swelling. No sounds that might whisper pneumonia or infection. Gentle pressure on the abdomen. That, too, is fine. Perhaps it is just a bout of stomach flu. Perhaps it will pass. Concern lingers just the same.

Now he sits down and does nothing. Without the eager technician to draw telltale blood or the modern machine to spit out a definitive prognosis of disease, the only tool he has today is his ability to see. Observation is a good diagnostic tool. He learned this trick over many years of medical practice. Truth be told, he still discovers more by observation than most young doctors glean with all their modern technological tools.

The exam seems to take forever. Everyone has left the room to allow him to have some privacy with his patient. Doctors generally do not like anxious daughters standing guard or speaking *for* the patient, particularly when the patients can speak for themselves. The small group makes small talk in the living room. I sit in Mom's chair. The rainbow quilt slips down behind my back.

"How's it going? I understand your husband is traveling a lot these days with the new job?" "Yeah, it's a real pain. He's beginning to regret taking it, but he is the firm's only lawyer licensed to practice in Indiana. What can ya do?"

"Do you think Mom will be OK? Easter is coming. She always likes Easter. She asked me yesterday when we were going to color the eggs. No one eats them anyway!"

"Do you remember the year Dad was so late for the holiday dinner? He went out to find some chocolate bunnies and all the stores were closed? Boy, was Mom steamed. She almost threw the ham at him." "And cousin Cheryl's wedding was the following weekend. We all had to tippy-toe around that family gathering, particularly when the groom's drunk brother showed up. Who knew what an idiot her fiancé was? No wonder the marriage didn't last." An awkward pause. The conversation turns back to the situation at hand.

"When is the doctor going to be finished? Is she dying? Is she just sick with a passing illness? I think we are all exhausted." "She has looked bad all day." "Why is he in the room so long? We offered her food this morning, tried to keep her comfortable, but mostly she has slept restlessly through the day."

The doctor came out, finally. Nothing about his expression appeared definitive. "What's going on?" my sister asks. We recognize a sober dread in his face.

"Not clear. I cannot find any evidence of anything new that might signal the coming of death. She's on only a few meds, as you know. There is no underlying diagnosis that indicates that death is imminent. On the other hand, she looks as if this may be the end. I'm sure that's both unwanted news and a relief for you, but . . . ."

They press him. "So, should we call the rescue squad? Is it time? Do we send her to the hospital? I know that last time she was hospitalized she said she never wanted to go again. [There was that unpleasant incident with her roommate.] But she's our mother. Don't we have to do everything?"

"There isn't much the hospital can offer. Let her rest and see what happens. And you folks try to get some rest."

Everyone is quiet. Everyone hurts. Everyone must watch and wait.

Two days later the wait is over.

> "tho' I'm not beside you
> still my love will guild you
> Goodnight, sweetheart, goodnight."

Death

The Birthday Party

"There's a garden, what a garden
Only happy faces bloom there.
And there's never any room there
For a worry or a gloom there."

("BEER BARREL POLKA," VACLAV ZEMAN, 1934)

EVEN AS WINTER'S SHADOW comes, dandelions reproduce themselves happily across the small yard, cheering the old green house. It is sturdy clapboard with a generous porch—built to last. The pathway to the back door is steep, much too difficult to navigate for the centenarian who lives there. The driveway shows signs of use, thanks to rotating caregivers and family who visit frequently. Although the yard is not neglected, it lacks the vibrant attention characteristic of vigorous, younger owners. No random baseballs or forgotten scooters clutter the quiet. No flats of tulip bulbs lie near barren beds waiting to be tucked in before winter comes.

The house is reaching its use-by date. Steep steps lead from the back door into a tiny but efficient kitchen. For me the first floor brings back memories and smells of holiday visits to a bevy of aunts long dead, those who hosted family gatherings with abundant food and good will.

Inside the living room photographs bloom in every space. They chronicle the history of a rich life. Three generations of a close and abundant family populate the walls, tables, and the kitchen bulletin board. The most impressive is a panoramic photo of the entire Catholic community of a now-defunct inner-city parish, founded in the early twentieth century to accommodate the growing Hungarian population in Cleveland. The picture sits proudly on the piano that dominates the living room. The entire congregation, grandparents to tiny children in their Sunday best, smiles in black and white at an ancient camera. Near the front of the assemblage is a small girl named Emma. Now an aging widow, she was a member of the growing immigrant community who processed that day from temporary quarters in a Benedictine monastery to the newly-built church, where they would celebrate its first Mass and the American dream. In the photo Emma is five. She is smiling.

A pile of scrapbooks rests on a small table in the corner. Emma spent many hours documenting the history of her parish and the stories of her children's lives. Each book is full of photos, a snippet of text, and a generous dollop of love.

The living room, too, is a snapshot set in time. Its caption: "Welcome." There is a place for everyone. Cozy afghans embrace two plump sofas. In the corner of the larger one there perks a small pillow, patched together with love from a robe Emma's daughter wore before she died two years ago. The robe was originally a wedding present from mother to daughter, a special gift for her wedding night. Emma likes to clasp the pillow close. It holds memories of that only daughter, who cared for her for many years. Whenever Emma hugs the pillow, she mourns her first-born. A tear drizzles down her cheek, releasing some of her pain.

Dominating the space is the vintage spinet, converted from an old player piano. So-called "barrel pianos" were popular early in the twentieth century. They were powered by a hand crank, which turned the barrel that produced the music.

Younger Emma was not dependent on a barrel to produce music. She played an ordinary piano for parish church gatherings and accompanied soloists for rousing social events. She loved to accompany family and friends as they sang—often in harmony—vintage songs. They loved: "Beer Barrel Polka," "Why Do I Love You?," "Moonlight Bay." In recent years arthritis drained the talent from her fingers. Even an energetic barrel turner could not bring it back. She continued her interest in music, though, composing her last piece, a polka, at 102 years of age. She can still retrieve the words to old songs and sing softly along when the family gathers for a party.

Plants big and small nestle on the sunny window seat between sturdy built-in cabinets in the dining room. The cut-glass windows shine. Emma's daughter-in-law, Karen, makes sure no part of the home, nor its resident, is neglected.

Many houses constructed in the early 1900s had such china cupboards flanking windows. The window seat between allowed visitors to chat comfortably close to the Christmas buffet set out on a generous table. There was turkey, fresh *csoroge* dusted liberally with powdered sugar, and homemade poppy seed roll, soft and savory.

Vintage family silver and special occasion plates, now seldom used, are stored in Emma's commodious cupboards. The plants are freshly watered. A vase of pink roses has been added, a gift for this gentle woman.

Today my brief pilgrimage to Emma's house is for a modest celebration to honor her birthday. After a person reaches one hundred years, every birthday is special. There will be a big family party next Saturday, with a home Mass. Ironically Saturday is the anniversary of the deceased daughter's birthday.

The gathering is sparse: her sons and daughters-in-law, the daily caregiver, "those women who come every day," as Emma describes them, and me. Someone has ordered a take-out lunch from a nearby deli. Cupcakes serve as the birthday cake. There will be a real cake on Saturday. Emma wears a birthday tiara. It marks her special day. Just to make sure no one leaves hungry, though, there are brownies, homemade cream puffs, and some tiny cheesecakes. No one brought poppy seed roll. Emma can eat only soft food these days. Her appetite, like her current world, has shrunk.

Emma's older son must leave to attend a meeting. The caregiver has another client to visit. Karen and I are all the party that remain. I have been promised a sing-along. It's time now. Emma's daughter-in-law relocates the party to the kitchen. The room was remodeled by a previous owner to accommodate a more modern look than its original depression decor. Karen knows what she is doing. The reason for our move is that the kitchen is small, rendering the sound more easily contained and amplified. Emma's hearing is not what it used to be.

Although we are a miniature and rather pathetic trio at best, the singing is vigorous, if occasionally slightly off-key. It is evident that Emma's hearing has diminished even more since her last birthday songfest. Her slight lag from the rest of the chorus says this loud and clear. We finish with a rousing "Happy Birthday" to Emma. She smiles gently. We each give her a tender hug.

I have errands to run and dinner to cook. The weather promises freezing rain. Goodbyes follow and I depart. The celebration is over. It is time for Emma's nap.

Karen tucks Emma in and carefully arranges the blanket around her on the comfy sofa that serves now as a bed. It is harder and harder for Emma to rest comfortably. These days even her naps are troubled by disruptive dreams. Her daughter-in-law smooths her hair. A retired teacher, Karen has surprising skill at hairdressing. Once a week she comes to wash and curl "Mom's" hair. Even as her body betrays her just a bit more each day, Emma always looks good. Karen sees to it. There is no hint of nursing home neglect that characterizes some elderly people: the uneven part or tell-tale white at the hairline that marks a lack of attention to the person's graying hair or the harried schedule of underpaid workers. For Emma, a new blouse appears for a special event. Clothes are always carefully washed and pressed. Love is generous.

The house is quiet now. Later Emma will turn on the TV to watch her daily Mass. Her faith is strong; her body not so much. She rarely leaves the house these days. She can no longer walk. Her body is frail. Its bones fragile. It is much too cumbersome to move her in her wheelchair down the porch steps, into the car, and into the church for the Catholic ritual she loves so much. The last time she went out was for her daughter's funeral. She has lived long enough to lose a husband, a son, a grandson, and her only daughter. Two married sons remain. They live on the far side of town.

While Emma sleeps, Karen washes the dishes in the tiny kitchen sink. There is no dishwasher here. The kitchen, never expanded from its early twentieth century style, is too tiny to accommodate such luxury. Who would have conceived of a machine that washed and dried a family's daily dishes? That was the work of wives and daughters, or of servants for those with greater means.

Karen tries to be quiet, hoping Emma will rest well for a change. She puts away the remains of the small party and tidies the rest of the downstairs, hoping in the next few days to have time to set up the small Christmas tree. She has done enough for today. She is tired. Right now she needs a short rest, anticipating Emma's needs in an hour or two.

For the last week Emma has urged her to rummage around on the second floor to find and assemble the holiday decorations. She mentioned it more than once. Karen can't understand the urgency, since December is two weeks away. Nevertheless, she'll find time. Emma is insistent. And it would make her happy. Some early snow begins to fall on the leafless bushes in the front yard. Surveying her work, Karen waits for Emma to awake. Soon after that Karen can go home. It is a long drive to the other side of town. She will hand off to another member of the devoted family. Her brother-in-law will cook dinner for Emma, put her to bed, spend the night. He'll make the Hungarian goulash that Mom likes. There will be enough for leftovers. Maybe the tree can go up tomorrow. There will be time. It is too late today to begin that task. And Karen is exhausted.

We didn't know it, but this was the last celebration held in that house of caring. It was time. This year there would be no Christmas decorations. The tree never went up in Emma's welcoming home. She died two weeks later. Emma was 103.

Last Rites

"Oh, Danny Boy. . . .
And if you come, when all the flowers are dying
And I am dead, as dead I well may be
You'll come and find the place where I am lying
And kneel and say an 'Ave' there for me."
(FREDERICK EDWARD WEATHERLY)

IT WAS WINTER AND nearly dark. Shortly after we received the call from her daughter late that afternoon, we decided we had better go. We drove slowly along deserted back roads, squinting through the dusky fog. A late winter gale swirled the last hurrah of desiccated autumn onto the windshield. Were we in a horror film? Yes, I guess we were. At least it felt that way.

The parking lot was deserted. No need for a long trek in the cold. As we got out of the car, the wind chilled us to the bone. We walked the few minutes to the entry. Beyond the glass doors of the sprawling one-floor building it was clear that the main desk was unattended. There was a sign that promised valet parking, but no valet appeared. We were well beyond visitors' hours, and any expectation of someone to park cars was a chilly illusion.

A ghostly silence replaced the wind as we entered the modest suburban surgery center, a satellite of the main inner-city campus. As we walked through, trying to find some human life to direct us to Mary Ellen's room, it felt almost as if aliens had come in the night to abduct the entire staff, leaving a gift shop and the soda machine untouched. Apparently, aliens do not pause to refresh.

I suppose this should not have been a surprise. It was the weekend, when all surgical patients have been successfully cut, cared for, and dismissed with sufficient pain medication to avoid those middle of the night calls to the doctor.

We wandered the mouse maze of deserted halls for several minutes, looking for any live person not attached to monitors or tubes who could tell us where to go. Most medical facilities are wide awake all day and night. People in white, occupied with important tasks and traveling computers, bustle about. The hospital lights were on and the doors were passable, so in spite of the empty halls, probably the place was open. Our footsteps echoed in the empty halls, no one in sight. Did the alien kidnappers have their way with the staff? At last! Luck found us a solitary nurse bent over her charts. Fortunately, she worked in the wing where Mary Ellen was actively dying.

When we talked on the phone yesterday, she sounded so good. Mary Ellen seemed in an upbeat mood and feeling better. Another friend left just before I dialed Mary Ellen's cell. They spent the afternoon watching the women's basketball finals, cheering and sipping surreptitiously from the flask of scotch smuggled in by her provident lunching buddy. They giggled like school girls, proud of their deception. The friend even thought to bring breath mints, to hide any evidence lingering on Mary Ellen's tongue. That night, though, things went downhill rapidly.

The pneumonia that initially provoked the hospital admission seemed worse. Mary Ellen woke in pain. Technicians came to do their thing. The x-ray confirmed pneumonia's successful invasion of the entire lung.

Mary Ellen decided well before this hospital admission to forgo any additional aggressive treatment. She was admitted to the hospital three times over the last six months. She was tired of dramatic trips to the emergency room—why do we always use the verb *rushed*? The cumbersome admissions process is anything but speedy: hurry up and wait, hurry up and wait.

She concluded she was done with her white-walled, contracting life: friends dying off, predictable menus in the restaurants she frequented with those companions who were still able to drive. (Did she really want another Caesar salad with chicken strips, dressing on the side?) She could no longer bowl, her favorite exercise and another social outreach. Not only were her bowling buddies becoming increasingly frail, Mary Ellen herself found her own ability to balance markedly diminished. She pictured herself lying in the alley someday ("lying in the alley," like a homeless person!), the oblivious ball rolling cluelessly toward the center pin (probably a strike!). Sitting sessile in a hospital bed for even a few days does not improve balance or strength, particularly as one ages. Besides, every item on her bucket list was all checked off. Why stick around like a past-its-prime pot full of mother-in-laws' tongue?

Her children urged her to move nearer to where they lived—a six-hour drive away, in a small town with no regular plane service. Away from a big city, though, their remote location offered a selection of stately retirement homes where older adults could play bingo, binge at ice cream socials with new friends, and receive the supportive services the aging process requires. Her daughters made visits to every one of the homes and selected three that they believed might appeal to Mary Ellen. They loved her very much and really wanted her to be happy and have a long life. While it might be costly to place mom in a terminal facility, that might be the best thing for her. They would manage.

Mary Ellen appreciated the wisdom of their wishes. She saw their concern in worried eyes. She did not want to be a drag on them or on her local friends, her old bowling buddies—or what was left of them! Yet since November her requests for help increased: "Could you drive me [she religiously avoided the term *rush*] to the ER?" Once even her long-time window washer called 911 for her. He watched her faint through a soapy window and rushed in to help.

The whole recurring enterprise had grown onerous, to friends and family certainly, and especially to her. Nevertheless, she hoped never to be a burden. She did not want her life, however lifeless it had become, to be a mere anorexic appendage to those about whom she cared.

The daughters were busy. They had husbands, children, active professional lives. Mary Ellen observed how families of her friends now living in assisted living facilities gradually eased minutes from their visiting time. How excuses to skip the visits multiplied.

Her friend Nora, herself installed in such a "home," described the reality. It happened over time. At first lots of people came. After that, only the faithful few continued to sign the visitors' log. Gritted teeth encased in forced smiles signaled how reluctant they were to repeat the ritual trips: not much to say, not much to make better. Good services from strangers, even in the best of homes, was not the same as family. Mary Ellen noticed tears form on Nora's face as she talked about her situation. Mary Ellen knew that Nora put on a different face, a happy face, when her family visited.

The last time she was admitted to the hospital, Mary Ellen vowed that it would be her *last time*. Determined, she made the decision. No standard advance directive form for her. She crafted a carefully detailed document as to what she wanted, and didn't want, if she became unable to speak for herself. She distributed copies to daughters, doctors, and close friends. There would be no ambiguity. She had already given up attempts to quit smoking: rationing, electronic cigarettes, finding other things to do when the urge persisted. She stopped going to water aerobics. She gained ten pounds. If she were going to die, she might as well die happy—and not smelling of chlorine! Meanwhile she began to gift close friends with her belongings: a pair of red sunglasses to a friend who loved red ("I just bought a new pair"); a favorite book to another ("I had an extra copy"). Was this with purpose? Did she want to leave a piece of her memory when she was gone?

This time antibiotics no longer were enough ammunition against her recurring infections. A body compromised by age and years of smoking found it difficult to resist battalions of determined bacteria, reinforcements multiplying by the hour. The patient was weary of the battle. She invoked her elaborate advance directive: no more. Her internist was reluctant to stop treatment, but she respected the patient's right to refuse. And now the germs cried victory! All territory and borders of Mary Ellen's lungs were securely occupied by the tiny, merciless creatures. She surely would die within a day or two. Family were notified and began the long drive in. They hoped to get there before the end, to spend with their mother the parsimonious piece of her life that remained.

Just before she slipped into that in-between time preceding death, Mary Ellen requested her church's last rites. The local pastor was called. He arrived a few hours before the family, read the prayers, anointed her, sang to her. Although she no longer opened her eyes or responded to questions from nurses or visitors, his arrival seemed to bring her back a little. She prayed along, answering the ritual prompts of the priest. When he finished the familiar ceremony, he closed the sacred book and began the Irish ballad, "Danny Boy." She smiled weakly. It was the most animated she was all day.

After he left, the family, exhausted from a long drive, arrived. Everyone settled in for the vigil. We knew it would not be long. Breathing became more labored. Extremities seemed cold, even in the warmth of the room. Mary Ellen was bundled in layers of blankets and sheets—a veritable laundry basket of linen! The night nurse came in to check her, to smooth the bed and the patient with relaxing medication. Breathing slowed, calmed by the nearness of death and the nudge of pain pills. Clearly, it was time.

In the deserted parking lot snow continued to fall. There was silence all around the hospital. Inside it was still as well. Mary Ellen stopped breathing at around three in the morning. Her cold hand grew limp in that of her older daughter. Some of the family—the children mostly—wanted to touch her, to kiss her one more time. Others simply turned away. There were sniffles from a few, frank tears from some, inane comments from others. "She is in a better place." (Yes, but we'd rather she were here.) "She looks so peaceful." (Well, she *is* dead, you know.) "She lived a good life." (True. In fact, she lived an exemplary life, caring for a dying spouse whom she detested and pouring out her care in volunteer work at her church. She read to the first-grade children, prepared the second grade for first communion, and played the piano for ten o'clock Mass every Sunday. She called her grandchildren religiously every weekend, listening to their recitation of dance lessons, pictures drawn, field trips to local museums.) One of the younger grandchildren tiptoed over to the bed, urging Grandma to wake up. She was too young to understand; puzzlement dammed away sadness. We cried.

There was little more to say or to do. The hovering band turned away and filed out. It reminded me of my own grade school daily dismissal, when each day the principal, Sister Blanche, said to the homework-laden eighth grade class, "Pass on." And each day we impudent students with scant experience of death, made our own joke about those words. Under our breath we added, "and go to Johnson's." Johnson's was a local funeral home that donated to the school heavy paper covers with advertising on them. Reused from year to year, loaned textbooks stayed nearly new when protected by Johnson's ads. "Pass on," on Sister Blanche's lips, always sounded to us like an invitation to choose death, expedited by the funeral folks. Johnson's tucks your books into sturdy covers. In due time, they tuck your loved ones into sturdy coffins. What did we know then about death?

On this too-early Sunday morning at this suburban hospital a grieving group left this curious classroom with fresh and sober knowledge. They walked out slowly, weighted down with heavy homework. It was time to prepare for the after-work of death.

The long halls remained dead quiet. Few patient rooms were occupied on weekends. As the small procession passed, signs on the doors of empty rooms assured them: "This room has been sanitized and is ready for use."

By Monday a new wave of patients would be installed, attended by staff and concerned families. The cubicle in which Mary Ellen died would join the cortege of "sanitized and ready" rooms. Hopefully the new tenants would walk out of the hospital whole. Perhaps they would not.

Outside night clung to its last few hours. It was still dark and dank. A chill slammed against the mourning group. The fog had not abated. Its thick, moist cloud hung over the sprawling rural landscape, much as it did over the family.

Inside the somber room, activity becomes brisk. The crew of professionals enters to perform their own "last rites." The fragile plastic tube that provided Mary Ellen comforting oxygen as she struggled to breathe is removed from her body with gentle care. The nurses place it with other items left over from the life that no longer needs them: rumpled plastic pads, a soiled gown, limp latex gloves, some wet tissues mangled from use. The exact time of death is noted on the chart. The body is removed; the bed is stripped of its scatter of sheets, blankets, pillows. The dirty dishes of death are never left to crust overnight with fluids or feelings of regret. Efficiency rules in this empty place. Perhaps it is a way for the professional care givers to clear away the painful reality of what they face each day. Busyness distracts from sadness and loss. It fills the head and heart with something that seems useful, especially when what one really wishes for is beyond human control.

The funeral home fetches the body, shrouds it in somber plastic. Johnson's of preteen giggles went out of business long before plastic body bags. What cover did they use to shield onlookers from that potent reminder of what was eventually everyone's fate? Does not Genesis 3 remind us of the ubiquitous legacy of primordial sin? Later the doctor will sign the death certificate. Paperwork must be served. Everything is official: jot and tittle. The doctor, too, will grieve a long-time patient.

Back at Mary Ellen's house, the family gathers in the newly renovated kitchen. Since the death of her husband, Mary Ellen has not cooked. The kitchen is pristine, except for a recently opened carton of cigarettes forlorn on the counter. In the living room, companioned by the television remote, is the missing pack.

One daughter wanders into the bedroom. Hanging on the closet door is a bag fresh from the dry cleaner. It contains the clothes Mary Ellen picked out several months ago to be her last outfit. The bed is made, corners carefully tucked. Slippers stand at attention at its side. On the dresser, there is a small box labeled "open immediately." It contains a list of bank numbers, safety deposit information, the will. Mary Ellen even remembered to jot down the name and phone number of the real estate broker with whom she wanted to list the house. Clearly death was not a surprise visitor.

No need to pick out the casket. Mary Ellen wanted to be cremated. She already selected a simple urn. A memorial Mass will be celebrated in her honor. When the weather permits, her ashes will be distributed on the grave of her abusive husband—a small irony. Life passes on.

Bertha

"When I grow too old to dream, your love will live in my heart."
(OSCAR HAMMERSTEIN II, 1934)

SHE NEVER WORE A bra and voted religiously for any woman who appeared on the ballot in those feminist-frugal days. She was among the first twentieth-century women to bob her curly hair, convenient when she took a dangerous spin clutched to the running board of a Model T. "Unorthodox" described her perfectly—one might say, to a T.

Maybe her early home life nourished her rebellion. When he drank, which was most of the time, her father chased her around the kitchen with a knife. He blamed her for the loss of an older brother. Her mother was pregnant with Bertha when the boy died unexpectedly before his first birthday.

The family moved a lot, a small caravan following the ups and downs of Pennsylvania coal mines. After the coal mines closed, her father worked only sporadically. Her mother cleaned other people's houses to keep food on the table. Some of the older daughters took on domestic work as well, helping contribute to the family. They scrambled to find the key to escape: a husband. The youngest, a boy, became a drunk in the likeness of his dad.

Bertha was the second last of nine, always the also-ran child. The nuns compared her negatively to the older sisters. Undaunted, after high school she managed to earn enough money to pay for one year of college. Immigrant families of that generation might scrape to send a son to college—rarely a daughter. If they did, the usual goal was an Mrs. degree, not a career. After her death, her daughter found a dusty first-year Italian book lay neglected on an old bookshelf. For Bertha there was never a second year.

Even after she married, at the geriatric age of twenty-seven, Bertha continued to get the short end of the family stick. Her house was never as perfect as were her siblings', nor was her outspoken daughter. Sometimes even celebratory family gatherings were strained. After the holiday meal, whenever the hosting sister offered homemade Christmas nut roll to take home; Bertha always got the dry, end piece.

Perhaps the siblings' attitude reflected the father's disdain for their little sister. Perhaps they resented that she married up, as they say. She and her husband, a college-trained professional, loved each other very much. Pictures show them holding hands, gazing into each other's eyes. They married during the Depression, in the first bloom of natural family planning for Catholics. Even so, three years later their union produced their only child, a daughter.

Bertha was never a joiner. The PTA and the Altar and Rosary Society were of no interest. Other than command performances, she skipped social events. In the chaos of a large family, she learned to survive in a personal private bubble. And she was happy to do so for the rest of her life.

Even after marriage, she kept as low a profile as possible. For the first struggling years during the Depression, she worked part time in a library. Starting a dental practice in a contracted economy is not easy, so she assisted in her husband's office. Dressed in the crisp white uniform of a dental assistant and seemingly only a part of the background, most of the patients never knew she was his wife.

She burned all the love letters sent from her husband while he was in the Navy. Her only daughter watched with regret as this precious history curled into ashes. But she understood that these were her mother's letters, after all, hers to dispose of as she wished. Bertha read them one by one for the last time, before she yielded the secret stories of her life to the flames.

During her early twenties Bertha kept a diary. After she died it was one of the few personal treasures that remained, squirreled away in her prized Art Deco cedar chest. Although she always claimed proudly to be well and happy, the diary confesses to her "feeling blue," apparently a euphemism for the depression she could not own.

Comfortable within her own protective skin, it was easy to maintain her singular life: sleep in, do a few necessary chores, read, watch television. And the men in her family were not the only members of her family who found solace in a bottle and a pack of Chesterfields. She ended each day with a couple of glasses of cheap muscatel. The wine came by the gallon, and somewhat embarrassed by her habit, she smashed the large bottles before she deposited them in the garbage. Itchy reddened skin on her face prompted a rare visit to a doctor. When the dermatologist asked her if she drank, she confidently answered no. Later, when asked about this untrue statement, she asserted, "Oh, that wasn't a lie. He meant hard liquor, you know, whiskey. I drink only wine."

After she became a widow in her late fifties, she gave away her husband's clothes, sold his dental practice, took a deep breath, and went on with life. She lived modestly on a small monthly Social Security check. Although very little was left after she sold the practice, she needed nothing aside from food and enough to pay the utility bills. Even so, sometimes she searched for the twenty-dollar bills she knew her husband secured behind switch plate covers and wadded into the corners of drawers. He loved to hide money—just in case there was an emergency.

Her brother-in-law, worried about her being alone in what he deemed "a changing neighborhood," bought her a small handgun for protection. Bertha was not afraid. She never wed bullets to weapon. The former lay awaiting consummation in a small drawer in a living room table, the virginal weapon in the other drawer.

She never craved new clothes or trendy gadgets. Sometimes she salved her widow's grief by listening to old records. Their dated melodies recalled how she and her husband danced, hosted silly costume parties, and survived the Second World War as a Navy family in hurricane-alley Florida. For many years she dreamed of her husband holding her as they waltzed to big band music at officers' parties. He sported his navy uniform, its lieutenant commander stripes sharp and clean. She wore a fashionable black crepe dress with a sequined pattern in white at the waist and the large shoulder pads of the era. She never lost her figure or her poise.

Several years into her widowed life, it became clear that she was not eating properly. She was admitted to the hospital for a short time to build up her weight. Reluctantly she agreed to move in with her daughter's burgeoning family. In this noisy new environment she found ways to be useful, to survive. While she was not able to do heavy work (a small stroke left her unsteady) she helped around the house, ironed the family's clothes, encouraged her grandchildren (as she had her daughter) to be independent.

When the parents were away, she tucked the children into bed. She sang to them as she had her own daughter. She loved to tell them stories as they grew heavy with sleep. She imagined a flowered meadow, a lovely summer bed for her granddaughter, whose pillow case was decorated with yellow blossoms.

And she kept her peace. Although she gave up her dog—the daughter's family already had one who did not yield an inch of his terrier territory—she could not bring herself to sell her house. It remained for her a symbol of independence. Someday, when it was time, she planned to move back in.

One day she offered to sort some test papers for her teacher daughter. She got them alphabetized quickly and went to return them, feeling satisfied that she could do something to help. Because her hands were full and her gait unsure, she slipped, falling on a newly waxed kitchen linoleum. It happened three days before her seventy-second birthday. The rescue squad came; an ambulance ride followed. Surgery, the repair of a broken hip, the anxiety of what-now? followed.

The doctors, optimistic, prescribed a nursing home for rehab. Bertha was less sanguine. As they came in to visit, the family found her in the darkened hospital room. Her arms clutched protectively around her body, her eyes and spirit were downcast and she was silent. In her internal narrative, "nursing home" meant life on the shelf, no autonomy, and being done. Nursing homes were where people go to die. The family agreed to take her home.

Since both her daughter and son-in-law worked, they hired a daytime care giver during the week. Bertha insisted that she would pay. She didn't want her daughter's family to carry yet another odious burden. Each week she wrote a check in her shaky script. Her writing could no longer achieve the perfect Zaner-Bloser method she learned from the nuns. Her monthly check was just enough to cover the cost of the care.

The arrangement worked for a while. Anna May came each day, her capacious body poured successfully into professional attire. She was cheerful and industrious, encouraging Bertha to engage, move, and get better. As she always did, Bertha charted her own course. She would have none of it.

Finally, after several bedridden months, she made the decision: it was time. It was clear, although she never said so, that she was determined to die. She decided not to go on. She worried that the cost of her care would exhaust whatever funds remained in her account. Her religion did not condone a decision to end a life proactively, such as with pistol or pillow pushed over the face. Resolute, she stopped eating instead.

The family tried to dissuade her. Her favorite foods arrived at her bedside at each meal, with company. No one likes to eat alone. Her daughter sat and chatted, encouraging her to take a bite or two. The grandchildren sometimes joined her, perched on the bed, tales of their school day tumbling out onto the covers. She entered their conversation, listening intently and offering comment, but she did not eat. Even attempts at assisted feeding were rebuffed. "Here, Mom. Your favorite. Try it." She smiled, took a tissue, and gently removed the food from her mouth.

Four months passed. She continued to take modest measures of liquid. She continued to refuse any solid nourishment. It was clear that she was in total control of her decision—no sign of dementia or depression. Predictably, she lost more weight from her already diminutive body. She began to resemble the granulated black and white pictures of liberated concentration camp survivors. Her daughter put on fifteen pounds. The disappearing woman posed a question to a friend, "Why is this taking so long?"

The family considered options: a feeding tube, medication that might perk up her mood and point to some life meaning for her. A relative, Uncle Harry, lived a pleasant and profitable life for four years after he consented to a permanent PEG tube inserted in his stomach to provide artificial nourishment. Bertha would benefit, even thrive, read again to the kids before bedtime. After all, she was barely in her seventies. Today people don't die in their seventies. There are treatments, surgeries, and pills to pile up bonus years.

Look at that ninety-five-year-old woman next door. She remained in her own home despite the wheelchair and the need for constant care. Look at all those smiling faces of truly elderly people on the brochures of nursing homes, or on television enjoying a tall glass of Ensure with happy and devoted daughters! They survived; so could Bertha.

Maybe a visit from a psychiatrist. Do they make house calls for bedbound old ladies who won't eat their spinach—or oatmeal or a proffered chicken wing? There has to be a medicine for this! Surely Bertha could be tricked or forced into taking a happy pill and begin to eat again. Aren't there medications for depression that stimulate appetite? After all, her family loved her. She shouldn't just give up. Wasn't this suicide?

Everyone continued to reassure her that her presence was a blessing and not a burden. The grandchildren joined the chorus. Anna May tried gallantly to twist her arm, or at least make it hold a fork. When the adults were at work, she cooked her excellent fried chicken. Even someone swooning contentedly after a hearty meal might find it hard to resist the siren smell of that great Southern specialty.

But Bertha did. From the time she was a child, the life map Bertha followed was not that of her parents—or of anyone else. She missed her husband. She missed her mobility. In the end the family yielded to her wishes. Forced intervention might destroy the meager autonomy that Bertha still held so tightly.

Death by denial of a thousand rejected meals takes a long time. It is difficult to watch. On her resolute path to that destination it took this tiny woman nearly five months to deplete her body's strength.

She died on a sunny day in August. It was near the anniversary of her husband's fatal heart attack over ten years before. The family was away the day Bertha died, a weekend break from watching her diminish day by day. They had sandwiched into the family van and visited an amusement park five hours away. The children rode the roller coaster and gobbled up hotdogs and cotton candy. At the end of each day they stopped for ice cream—two scoops and a cherry—on the way back to the motel. The parents, worried, spoke each day with Anna May. She assured them Bertha was about the same. They called one last time on the way home. They were just two hours away.

Bertha knew they were coming. It was time. She took one last deep breath. Death brought a peaceful relief.

This Is My Body[1]

"The Word became flesh and made his dwelling among us. . . ."
(THE GOSPEL OF JOHN)

THEY DRAW THE CURTAIN as the technician removes the ventilator, bowing to the patient's advance directives. Breaths come in labored punctuation to the prayers for the dying. The black-clad priest says the words of the Catholic sacrament and blesses the body of his departing brother: "Through this holy anointing may the Lord in his love and mercy help you with the grace of the Holy Spirit. May the Lord who frees you from sin save you and raise you up." The ritual action is complete.

At the bedside, the gathered weep, and lay down their goodbyes. Some touch briefly the pale and peaceful hand; others pause and bow their heads in a final prayer. Modern science, repentant, waits outside the *Shekinah* of the divine will. It has no power here. We wait. We wait. But it is not yet time. The patient is transferred to a nursing home.

Three weeks pass. Breathing is less labored. A steady procession continues to come and go. Friends and family enter the sterile nursing home room in silent steps. They need not worry that their entrance will wake him. The dying priest lingers in an irreversible coma. Not-yet-mourners come. Some linger. All await his final Eucharist.

Hushed conversation around the bed is future-driven, speculating how long it will take for the pneumonia to claim its prize. Some talk is retrospective, paging through the leaves of this man's life from the chapters before technology inflicted both hope and despair. Some say nothing.

1. Originally published in *Emmanuel*. Used with permission.

As a bioethicist, I have watched this kaleidoscope of feelings at many bedsides. As a good friend of the patient, all my dispassionate professional discussions about ordinary and extraordinary, active and passive, dissolve. Here they become flesh in the wasting shell of expiring personhood.

After Mike died, I recorded these paragraphs on my computer. The intention was to incorporate them into a scholarly article revisiting the question of active euthanasia. Now it seemed so irrational: to stand impotent at the scene of the now-regretted effect of human resuscitative intervention. From the onset, there was little hope of survival.

It seemed wrong not to bear the responsibility to undo this well-intentioned but poorly thought-through human action. If resuscitation were not initiated, this friend, who helped so many others to die peacefully and well, would himself have died that way. He would have realized his wish of never living in a vegetative state. He said, "If this ever happens to me, put a bullet through my head."

Was it morally right for those who saw him fall, his heart fail, to intervene? Is it morally right for us to avoid responsibility for such actions with a pious abdication, "It is now in God's hands?" It was not God who hoped to deprive death its prize with hopeless borrowed breath impressed on the still figure lying on a cold gym floor.

What I chose to write instead seems to have little to do with bioethics. Scholarly musings do not lessen pain or bring back a friend. In retrospect much more happened at this sorrowed bedside than an anguished decision to "pull the plug." The experience of a month's vigil showed me this truth. It no longer seems fitting to address the moral rightness of such an action without emotion, to speak in theories and with academic weight, to write reality into careful casuistry. Rather, it is much more appropriate to recount what was seen and heard at the bedside of this dying priest, and to tell the deeper story of a final Eucharist.

In the beginning the God of Genesis held a mud-made man and smiled in admiration. God breathed into its nascent nostrils. The still form moved with life. Today priestly hands lift the quotidian bread of consecration and breathe the ensouling words: "This is my body given for you. Do this in memory of me." Animated bread is lifted up from its golden plate and rested on a cross-signed cloth.

A hospital bed covered in a larger cloth offers up a wasting body, sustained beyond tubes and technology for the gathered group to see. Each labored gasp of air expires in view of those who watch. But watching grows weary. Those who linger vigilantly through days and nights tell stories to pass the time, to re-member deeds and parables from sixty years of living. The stories comfort and bring together not only the pieces of his life but this sober community.

This is my body. Here on the hospital patin the priest with sparkling eyes no longer teases and laughs, no longer responds with wit and wisdom to the gentle cues of others. *This is my body.* Now hot with fever, now sleeping or yawning, this body prompts a futile joke among the gathered: perhaps the patient finds the conversation boring. Yet each knows the unspoken truth that this fallow, pillowed mind no longer has the capacity to be bored. Closed eyes shroud forever the teasing twinkle.

This is my body. This is a friend's body, touched now by tears. It is a brother's body, taken untimely from his kin. It is a patient's body, shrouded in white and sterile dignity, turned now and again to keeps its skin-sheath unbroken. *This is my body,* broken. *Do you not yet understand?* John's Gospel words scent the air with Christian hope.

Body given for you, blood and breath exchanged for always life. Visitors at the bed remember stories of a life lived in service. A family holds each other tenderly. The young alcoholic, sober, weeps. The widowed mother comforts her grown sons and daughters, recapitulating the patient's care for them when they, as children, wept for *their* father.

No one comes who does not bring a story of kindness, of laughter, of meals shared and sorrows lessened. None enters without some gift, some fragment of life to lay on this altar of death. *Unless you die . . .* Word spoken and heard. Each one, hungry, gathers up what is offered, blessed, and shared: twelve baskets multiplied in memory. *When you do this, remember me.*

Eucharist is not a spectator sport. This bedded body stirs and breathes more deeply, and for a moment its motion recalls its former self. Attentive, the student nurse gently swabs the membranes of the congested mouth. Someone replaces the cold cloth on the forehead to ease the fever. Another hums an Irish song, purposed for the patient's ears but in truth sung to soothe the singer. The assembled attest that their pilgrimage is to honor the one stricken, but he neither hears their words nor feels their tender actions.

Those here to serve the fading life begin to minister to one another. Fingers stretch to touch the hand of the young student who stands helpless and weeping. A funny incident is recited and, for a moment, brings comfort. Photographs are retrieved to provide a morsel of memory of better times.

Do not cling to me, but rather go and tell everyone what you have seen, what you have heard, what you have touched. This event is true Eucharist, celebrated in this unlikely glass-walled space. Again, again, again, the ritual of death and life returns. We take and eat, we digest what we have eaten. Friends and family come hungry. All leave with bellies full not only of sorrow, but also of hope. *I will not eat or drink again with you until the kingdom.*

The white cloth drops from the forehead. The body ceases to breathe. It surrenders the final fragments of its spirit. Professionals process in to cleanse, to dress, to prepare the lifeless form to pretend one last time to hold life.

In the end its sturdy tabernacle is lowered into the earth, companioned with others who, believing, turned to dust before. *The hour comes when you will each go your own way, leaving me alone. Now it is finished.* It is time. The celebrant instructs the faithful, "Go in peace."

The Christ, who marked this fragile and sinful human being with God's own image and who promised him life beyond life, is not dead in the bodies or the memories of those who have come to see. Many have intersected with this redeemed and well-lived life, and having done so, will imitate in their lives his transubstantive incarnation.

One life lived well has greater meaning than a funeral tribute can speak. We who walk away, will we remember? Can we re-member, re-form this lifeless person tabernacled here and pass on to others that word of life joined and spoken in his concrete flesh? It's time.

Saying Goodbye

"If I cannot do what I want to do, I must want to do what I can do."

(LEONARDO DAVINCI)

AN AUNT OF MINE, a survivor of colon cancer, always ended her phone calls with, "Kiss the babies for me." I was in my thirties at the time, busy with those babies and disinterested in conversations about dying. Given her age and medical risks, Aunt Betty knew that any day might be her last. She might never have another opportunity to speak with her niece, her godchild. She made sure that, each time she did, she said her goodbyes. Medical checkups showed no evidence of the return of her cancer. As it turned out, though, there came a day when she *was* correct. Without warning, she died peacefully in her sleep. She was eighty-two.

Now nearing eighty myself, I have glimpsed the face of death. Two very dear friends died within the last five years. A third has Parkinson's Disease. Another good friend is a gaunt figure fading in his nursing home cubicle, an anthropomorphic Cheshire Cat as in *Alice in Wonderland*. Unlike the fictional feline, though, he rarely has a toothy grin or even a slight smile.

When do we say goodbye? We do not know, as the Gospel of Matthew cautions, "the day or the hour." Is this the last time we will offer a birthday toast at a favorite restaurant or play peek-a-boo with a grandchild? There was a student of mine in a life-long learning program, a widow, full of life. She registered for every class she could. Dressed to the nines, she chose a seat smack in the middle of the front row, so she would not miss a thing (or maybe so she could hear!). She drank up class content like a thirsty person guzzles water. She asked good questions, often connecting them to her life experience. She spoke about her trips around the world. She always came to class wearing bright colors and showy jewelry. And then one week she was not there. She had died a few days earlier just as she was leaving home for a luncheon date.

Her story could be a cautionary tale for ours. How do we shape choices in the final years, or perhaps months or days, before we cannot do so? Our death may surprise us and come without warning. We may move gradually "into that good night" preceded by months or endure years of erosion from disease. Perhaps the mind will melt away and leave only the carcass of the vital person who functioned once with awareness. "You do not know the day or the hour. . . ."

The waves of life's busyness wash over such existential questions, smoothing them away like sand castles on a beach. We make grocery lists, plan next year's vacation, or plump the pillows on that forty-year-old sofa. Like the biblical Martha, we are busy about many things. We rarely address how we want to spend the inevitable last days or moments.

When our attorney was preparing our wills, he cautioned that one's last illness can wipe out any remaining assets. That reality should be considered when making a will. I told him in jest that it didn't matter. Before that happened, I planned to die quietly in my sleep or send my wheelchair over a cliff. It is easy to deny what could be a prolonged process of dying: the incremental incisions of an insidious cancer, a slowly failing heart, or a stroke that does not kill. These are not scenarios ripe for a bucket list. Nevertheless, as one of my grandchildren loves to say, "Happens."

What parts of life need to be set in order, resolved, brought to closure or completion? First, one might consider practical or physical things. There is estate planning, of course. Telling the children where we keep our wills, bank accounts—or even the car keys—is important. I constructed a list of the "stuff" that so far resists removal from the house that for over forty years sheltered six children, a trio of large, sprawly dogs, a phalanx of fish, gerbils, and guinea pigs. List making gives a person a sense, or at least the illusion, of control. Death rarely does.

There are pieces of furniture about which I care deeply: my mother's secretary. It cost $29 during the depression. I still have the receipt! A Victorian love seat, made by a family friend as a wedding present for his bride early in the last century, rests regally near the front door. Twice it traded in its mourning black for a more contemporary coat. Its current outerwear is a cheery brocade with tiny cherries marching down the fabric.

Photographs my father took of the woods where he met my mother hang on the living room walls. While no jewelry of value waits for my daughters' eager claim, there are several pieces that my father created in the small laboratory behind his office. Each time I open my jewelry box, these treasures formed from love and dental gold bring him back to me. Maybe I should write that down. My children do not know the story. Will they care?

I make a concerted effort to deposit irreversibly decrepit debris into the garbage can. Basement cupboards are empty, the wrinkled artwork of six children is distributed either to their owners or to the recycle bin. I joke that, like my friend Ivy, I will leave my collection of empty cardboard containers. Local son, John, can pack them for Goodwill with any remaining junk. Maybe he can sell the neglected Fisher-Price toys on eBay. My father's collection of rusting nails (he died in 1968) waits patiently in peanut butter jars to turn a landfill iron-rich. I doubt that Meg's husband will want them for his restoration company.

At least I am the reigning sovereign over the state of my home. I organize, I sort, I glue descriptive signs on the backs or bottoms of treasures ("Ann drew this," "Michael did this in shop," "Dan made this in pottery class"). I'll throw away love letters that I want no one else to read. (Or should I save them?) I'll keep the memory book from Florence that Laura made.

I put off sharing my completed memoir with my children. Somehow not yielding its personal contents gives me jurisdiction over who I am, and perhaps over my life itself. Never mind that this is magical thinking.

Second, there are the people I want to see again before I die. There is always that friend that used to come to book club, the neighbor who remembers our promise to have lunch soon, the high school buddy whose 1955 Christmas card deserted its place in the dog-eared scrapbook and fell to the floor one day. There is no reason to glue it back again. The silly note inside gave me a good laugh. It will do the same for my friend. When will I call her?

Wouldn't it be good to have a few more cousins' "out to lunch" gatherings before we are all too old to drive? A four-hour session with wine and unwinding of decades of family tales is not a bad activity for three old ladies. Hurry. Weather and distance will displace plans. Is there a time when urgency becomes futility? Does time slip gradually through our fingers, like the sands in an hourglass—or in an instant, like that glass crashing to the floor?

I must remember to send the brittle 1940s photo to that little boy, now a retired chemist. He is smiling as he plants a kiss on his little friend, the one with whom he used to try to dig to China. The tender moment is fixed in time. We are dressed for Halloween. He is a Spanish *caballero* and I a Chinese princess, all glittery in cheesy store-bought blue rayon. The photo is black and white; our young lives were full of color and promise.

Third, maybe I should travel more. Brochures describing cruise tours and elder learning experiences pile up on my desk. Maybe. I know I want to see the ocean beach once more, to wiggle my toes in warm sand, search for that unique shell, and taste the salt on the breeze. I want to watch the sun slip beyond the waves, dragging the crimson aura of its golden disc into its reflection. This is best done with fingers entwined with my husband of over half a century. Is there time for this? Will he be there with me or I with him?

Each time I visit a place I love, I wonder if I will see it again. Thirsty, I drink in the hills of Tuscany, the lightning leaping from hill to hill in a drenching rain. I never want to lose that image. We will return to Florence yet again. The trip has become addictive, an annual pilgrimage. Time for one more intoxicating experience, even without the local red wine.

Cameos of new-made friends in the charming city on the Arno come to mind. There is the Israeli woman, in Florence to learn Italian. We watch her each day as she practices the language with the dining room staff. She is smartly dressed, as European women always are. No worn-down tennis shoes or tattered tank tops. One day we stop for a drink in the lobby bar and she is there, on the phone with a friend. She smiles and hangs up. We engage in a conversation. Over the next year we exchange emails. There are get-well wishes when her partner suffers a serious medical event, random recommendations of good books, expressions of hope that she might return to Florence this year. To see her again would be a blessing.

This year the person who first greeted us at the Florentine hotel—her name is the same as one of our daughters—will still be there. She will rush in early in the morning in time to change from fashionable street clothes to the formal staff uniform, ready to greet, to joke about going to jail for an accusation from a disgruntled guest, to wish us well. She will tell us all about her wedding. This year we missed seeing her. She was on her honeymoon.

We look forward to greeting the waiter in a local trattoria, the one who served a challenged man with humor and generosity. As the place was about to open, the man waited at the door. Hair slicked with water. Shirt neat and new. First in line. He was eager to sit down for lunch. Did this happen every day? The waiter joked with the man as he pretended to pour the wine (still corked) onto his plate instead of his glass. Both laughed. I don't think the waiter ever presented a bill. There are so many memories of that place, so much to be cherished and revisited in memory: a celebration dinner with our children and theirs, a long walk to the hilltop with the great view of the city, getting lost for an hour because we walked the wrong way in the rain. There are more memories to be made.

Regret always occupies a corner of one's suitcase on any return trip. The generous man who staffed the hotel desk died two years ago. The manager of the small hotel outside the city moved to a larger property in another city. The favorite museum, the one that houses Donatello's magnificent Mary Magdalene, is closed for renovation. To a large degree these instances provide a metaphor for the whole of life. Things and people we treasure most are not taxidermy effigies, souvenirs that we can unpack, display, and admire when we come home. They slip through our grasp and from our memories. Like the stilted horses on a carousel ride, they pass by quickly. The music stops. We must get off.

Will there be another trip to that tiny town near Florence? Can our aging bodies withstand the long flights or the cobbled streets of endless walking? Last time we visited, someone we had met on an earlier trip, an elderly Englishwoman whose Parkinson's had devoured her memory except for her ability to calculate points in a game of dominoes, died the week before we arrived. She and her husband, retired from the States to an apartment in rural Italy, came each warm evening to watch the sun set from the terrace of our hotel, a high spot in the little village with two tiny restaurants and a great view of rolling vineyards and gathering clouds. And that thunderstorm. I finger the gaudy pink ceramic heart on my dresser, a gift from the generous woman who ran one of the two local restaurants. Will we ever see her again?

So many years; so many people passing quickly by or taking root in our lives. I do not know if a heaven exists, but it would be wonderful to meet many of them again, to listen again to their lives, to linger with a glass of wine or cup of tea. People who populate our lives need to be held long and close.

Will I see my friend in a city on a river, whose name means life? When we first met, for business, she was forty and full of energy. Today her body is owned by the results of cancer, which seems to crave a fresh organ from her body as it exhausts another. We exchange emails, some funny, some sad; but there is no presence for hugs or laughter or to wipe away tears.

A lunch with a high school friend in Chicago. Four hours. She is a writer. We exchange portions of our recent work. We offer suggestions to improve them. Maybe the publishers will approve. We talk and talk. So much to say, memories and catch-up bits and pieces of life. She lost a son, likewise to cancer. Was she able to say goodbye to him? What did she say? Was it enough?

I spend time with my spouse: out to dinner, think about a movie, visit a museum. More and more our social life revolves around "special year" birthdays. Last weekend we were invited to an event for a divorced couple we have known for more than fifty years. Their birthdays are in the same month. Their children brought them together to celebrate eighty years each of life, albeit a life strained and stained with tears. Nevertheless, to see their children grown and secure, to hear their stories—what a lovely time! An unresolved issue caused a rift between the husband and my family. I'm not sure what could heal that! At the party the elephant remained tethered in the coat closet and did not bellow into the midst of the party.

Fourth on the bucket list—how many of us complete it?—is to say unspoken things: "I love you"; "here's a story you never heard"; "I'm sorry." My closeted memoir is certainly a part of that. When my husband read it, he was surprised that I never mentioned to him the time long ago that I considered taking my own life. Private, even scary thoughts are part of the consciousness we each carry. Mostly we carry them locked forever: words never spoken. And many of them are very heavy.

When my mother stopped eating, I knew that the larder of her life was almost bare. Several times I tried to have that "meaningful" conversation of goodbye. Most languages have many ways to put it: *adieu* or *adios*, go with God; *ciao*, both hello and goodbye in Italian; *sayonara*, more final than *ja mata* (see you later) in Japanese; *shalom*, the Hebrew parting wish of well-being or peace. Yet our goodbyes never quite intend to say, "I'll never see you again." I did not say a proper goodbye to my mother. As she had lived, she died without anyone close to her. Although she walked in the shadow of death each step of each day for the more than ten years after my dad died, we never spoke that forbidden word to each other.

If I speak of death now, am I not impertinent or politically incorrect? If I intend to say parting words truly for the last time, do I curse a relationship or the person to whom I say them? There are myriad ways to talk of death that never really use the word. Yet we all die, and it is real to face it.

In the end, we need to own our "goodbye" to the body in which we live. No matter the pills, the exercise, the magic of modern medicine, the body has its way. Telemeres, those little pieces and parts at the end of each chromosome, stop regenerating as they did when they were young. The efficient factory of our bodies begins to show the obsolescence familiar in industrial age workplaces. The vigor and speed of the teen years becomes the creak and ebb of age. The rust of age has its way.

I laugh when I see someone hold a small-print document at arm's length. The eyes of the forty-something don't focus well for close reading. Arms do not lengthen to aid a better view. Once I observed a woman trying to order her dinner in a lovely restaurant with "atmosphere" (aka "low-wattage lighting"). She must have been a smoker, because she retrieved a pack of matches from her purse. She lit them, one after another, trying to read the tiny words on the menu. I did not stay around long enough to find out if she had a few remaining matches to order dessert. Happily, we who were myopic from childhood have an edge in later life. The inability to read small print in dusky light is not so pronounced. Maybe we were born with longer arms!

Inevitably the body betrays us. Teeth that have been tenderly brushed and flossed for decades begin to crack. Gums recede, as if denying a long-standing friendship with the teeth that hold them close. The dentist, aging himself, laughs: "To be expected."

Fingers that could play rapid scales and Debussy intricacies develop minor aches and small bumps where flexibility used to be. Chubby toes a mother once counted to her young daughter ache in new shoes because bunions press against the sides. The nails are difficult to cut and difficult to reach—that need for longer arms again. Some nails may even harbor the newest terror threat: toenail fungus! (But at least for this affliction the commercial assures us there is a cure.)

Perhaps the worst is the sagging center, the reorganization of the main body. I have often joked that as we age, the breasts sag, the tight tush moves its comely curves to the front to create the belly, which itself droops over time. The punch line is, "When it all lies in a pile on the floor, then you die." Perhaps that's what happened to the Wicked Witch of the West: total meltdown!

Sometimes serious illness causes a permanent rift, literally. Two pale scars align my ventral side: the lower line chronicles the children birthed the way of Caesar; the upper reminds me of my rearranged vessels. The mammary arteries that helped provide nourishing baby milk have happily reinvented themselves to feed my heart. Coronary conduits aged out, clogged with decades of sludge. In the end, only specialized medical plumbers could provide a cure.

Men whose prostate gland is gone are reminded of the defect by difficulty motivating their manhood or by leakage from the urinary tract. Make peace. Say goodbye. Women who have undergone a hysterectomy cannot bear children. Make peace. Say goodbye.

In any case, one must leave behind youthful beauty, physical prowess, keeping up with the grandchildren in the annual Turkey Trot race. It's time to lie low and become like the Thanksgiving turkey: sessile and seasoned, but at least once a year the center of attention.

Most of the time the aging person is no longer expected to be the center of attention. Children, and sometimes even younger friends, help you on with your coat or across the street. Whether you need it or not! No one expects elder folks to have anything to add to a conversation, which often turns to the irrelevant pap of television celebrity or the latest fictional superheroes. Ideas gleaned from years of learning and experience are not valued when they come from mouths surrounded by wrinkles.

In my forties I had the occasion to interview the theologian who was the subject of my dissertation and a giant among the theologians of his time. Retired from teaching, he lived alone in a small house on the outskirts of a small college town. His corrugated iron garage door, protruding from the hill at the front of the property, was rusted and covered with weedy vines. He seemed to me to be of advanced age, probably at the time not yet eighty. As I sat in the sober black leather chair in his living room, he remarked, "During the [Second Vatican] Council bishops sat in that chair." (He was the wise voice of counsel behind such important documents as *Gaudium et spes*.) "Today, no one comes," he observed wistfully. At the time his comments resonated with nothing in my experience. Today I understand. Older people can say goodbye to their place as a relevant part of others' lives. "Retirement" renders you a disposable redundancy to the ordinary time of others. Nevertheless, as one of my daughters likes to say in the face of difficult things, "It's all good."

As we prepare for life's last hurrah, the instances of "goodbyes" multiply. We bid goodbye to things, to people we loved, to our own bodies, and sometimes to our memory. While we are still intact, we can decide whether we wish to do more while we are able. We can choose how we react to goodbyes about which we have no choice.

Will we ignore the mess of stuff and hurts that we may leave for others to deal with? Will our legacy be a hoard of junk and unfinished business? Do cardboard boxes wait, ready to receive them?

We may add to our bucket list: friends, new memories, perhaps a trip to Australia to bungee jump. We may decide whether to let the loose ends of our life remain frayed or to bind them up and grasp the precious moments before they slip from our cooling hands. What do I want yet to do? What do I yet want to say, before I can no longer say "good bye"? It's time.

A Process for Making Decisions

Name the Problem

PROBLEMATIC DECISIONS BECOME MORE complicated or even deadlocked by not clearly defining the dilemma, that is *a moral situation with several options but no single right answer*. In contains conflicting values, conflicting possibilities, conflicted people. A son thinks his mother ought to live forever. She says she is done with life. A daughter wants her frail father in a nursing home. Dad wants to stay at home. He says he doesn't care if he falls and dies in place—even if he lies there for days. And the siblings are just frustrated.

Identify the Decision-Maker

A good decision requires identifying whose decision it is. Medical decisions are complex; there is often more than one stakeholder. Ideally the patient or *person most affected should have the final say*. Concretely, if it is my life or my body, it is my choice to make. Persons have the right and responsibility to chart a life course that fulfills the values and hopes that define them.

When a person is competent, that is has *the capacity to understand here and now* the range of choices and their implications (burdens and benefits, possible side effects), she is the appropriate decision-maker for her medical or life care. That includes the right to refuse treatment, even generally accepted treatment. Only if she becomes incompetent, either permanently or for the time being, must someone else decide for her.

If the person is unable to make his own decisions, the law designates a line of "next of kin." This means that a spouse or a parent or an eldest child will bear that burden. Every competent person can, and should if he wishes, designate someone else to decide for him. This person becomes his voice, but only if he cannot speak for himself either temporarily or permanently.

There is no requirement that the designee be the next of kin or even a relative. It should be someone who shares the person's values, or at least *is willing to carry them out*. This designate is called the durable power of attorney for health care (DPAHC). The DPAHC has jurisdiction *only* in matters of health. If possible, a person who speaks both with authority and in the language of medicine is a good choice.

The doctor, the family, the guilty cousin in Colorado, the administrator of the hospital, the government, the basso-voice actor urging the trial of a miracle medicine, or even the revered Sean Hannity or Rachel Maddow do not qualify as appropriate decision-makers for an individual's well-being, or get to decide about medical intervention (unless, of course, that person is named as such on the advance directive form).

On the other hand, such people can exert an influence on one's choice. A doctor may have strong beliefs in favor of a certain treatment. The patient is reluctant to disobey expert medical advice, so she gives consent against her own values. A television commercial or celebrity expert may convince someone that a certain surgery or pricey pill always works.

Maybe a mother does not want bypass surgery, but she sees the look on her children's faces when she hesitates to sign the consent form. She may believe the procedure is too expensive, placing a burden on family or the common good. Perhaps she decides quietly to omit the news of a terminal cancer to her spouse. "I don't want him to worry."

There are times, also, when the arc of a personal decision must yield at the brink of others' interests and values. No matter how strong or reasonable one's wishes or arguments may be, they cannot force violation of another's conscience, law, or institutional policy. A doctor is not required to abort a pregnancy if she believes abortion to be morally wrong. Deadly firearms should not be part of the recommended treatment plan provided by those sworn to "do no harm." A hospital may have a policy that requires resuscitation if a patient heart stops during surgery. That policy would override a valid patient do-not-resuscitate order.

Even if a patient demands it, a hospital administrator ought not authorize futile treatment. Futile treatment from the provider's point of view is any intervention that is not effective in one of two ways. Either it does not achieve the required effect (a patient continues to bleed out even though multiple transfusions are given, for example), or it does not change the course of an underlying illness (a patient with metastatic cancer is actively dying and the family wants to continue medicine for high cholesterol). Many hospitals have written policies that detail what their institution defines as futile. It should be noted that treatment can also be defined as futile if the patient believes it does not correspond with the patient's values and expectations (the patient is ninety, has no bucket list, and refuses an antibiotic for pneumonia).

A patient may have to find another hospice facility, for example, if the one to which they are admitted does not provide the resuscitation he wants as part of his plan. A family cannot demand an intervention that the facility's policy or the law precludes. Continued chemotherapy on a cancer spread beyond the treatment's efficacy cannot be demanded. It is futile. Assisted suicide remains unlawful in most states.

One more thing should be noted. Laws can and should evolve, but good laws are based in human-worthy values, common consent, and the common good. In a liberal system, such as the United States', changes in law are best considered over time and with broad opinions of input.

Prepare the Document

When a person enters a hospital, usually someone in the admitting department will ask, "Do you have an advance directive?" This reminder affords an opportunity to construct one. Hospital personnel may be able to help, but not all personnel are trained to do this. The process does not require a lawyer, and standard forms, as well as laws, differ from state to state. The hospital may provide a form, but it is always better to think about this important document beforehand. Hospital admissions are rarely times for calm deliberation.

The ideal advance directive should contain as much detail as the person thinks necessary. Do I want to be resuscitated? Would my medical condition before the event make a difference? If I am demented and refuse to eat, do I want spoon feeding or artificially assisted nutrition? If I'm old and sick, do I want antibiotics for my pneumonia? These choices require serious consideration of one's preferences and consultation with others.

The best document is the one prepared long before urgency forces the issue or regrets its neglect.

The final consideration concerns the application of existing law. Certain states may require special protocols before a patient's written wishes to die a natural death without further intervention can be honored. Some require that the wish to forgo resuscitation be defined clearly and on a standard form.

Laws may dictate the actions of others. A hospice team cares for a person who is clearly not safe at home. The team is bound, by law, to report such conditions. This is true even against the protestations of a competent patient. Dilemmas of this sort must be parsed with care. The attempt must be made to balance the values and wishes of the patient against those of the law.

Identify the Relevant Facts

The key task is to *avoid cluttering the decision process with data that has no relevance to the heart of the decision*. In difficult cases, extraneous information clouds the process. Is the decision dependent on influenced by whether the decider is tall or rich, assertive or compliant? Does it matter that the patient loves doughnuts or prefers sparkly shoes? Whether Mr. Smith is a nice elderly gentleman who likes figs and gives money to charity, or had an affair once when he was seventeen, are not criteria as to whether he should be in hospice or on a transplant list. These accidental facts are not relevant.

Among the important facts in medical decisions are what the suggested treatment or resolution entails, how well it works. This includes an explanation of side effects, an assessment of risks and benefits, presented in an understandable manner. It entails a *clear understanding of the consequences of the action under consideration and other possible solutions*. Only then can a person give *informed* consent. It may require an estimation of cost (financial as well as emotional), although that consideration should be more the choice of the patient than that of any professionals. Health care and human well-being are not consumer products. Rather, they are rights intrinsic to the human person.

Name and Prioritize the Values Involved

What values can and should be realized? Moral dilemmas *are* dilemmas precisely because the situation has *embedded values that are in competition and conflict.* Radiation may have debilitating side effects that preclude normal activities during a long course of the treatment. Will this treatment extend my life longer than the quality of life I lose while receiving treatment? Curative surgery may require anesthesia that is risky for some, or it may leave disfigurement for others.

A nursing home provides safety, but it also removes a degree of autonomy. The resident cannot play loud music that disturbs others or may not be able to continue to pursue an oil painting hobby, because the toxic fumes are harmful to lung-compromised patients. Either might be an annoyance or a health risk for a resident with allergies. Independent living facilities may require a resident to wear a name badge.

The cost of surgery without insurance might bankrupt a person. Is it worth losing my home and life savings to undergo expensive therapy? Perhaps it will buy someone only a few months more of life and make the children happy. It that goal more important that a lesser time without the side effects of the course of treatment?

Most morally difficult situations are laden with competing values. Time lost to pursue a good outcome vies with length of treatment, autonomy argues with safety, cost wrestles with cure. Sometimes the competing values of the multiple stakeholders muddy the issue even more. In the best scenarios, priorities of the decision-maker should be given preference.

The *values of the patient* come first, but sometimes only to *pursue* his wishes. In some instances I have no entitlement to something or some accommodation (a mansion that I cannot afford or a liver transplant when I'm actively drinking), but only the right to try to work to attain these goals. (Save my money for the house or be sober for the prescribed time.) This is called a *negative right*, that is the fulfillment of some goals does not incur a responsibility for others to help them be realized. This is especially true if those goals counter others' values (asking someone to assist in suicide, for example). It remains a good idea to express expectations and wishes in written form and in conversations with one's designated decision-maker. Not only does this provide a reasonable guarantee for having one's wishes observed, it lessens the burden of deciding for the surrogate. The daughter who must decide whether to remove life support does it more easily if her mother has made that clear ahead of time, ideally in written form. Advance directives try to consider every possibility, but at the heart of a person's choices are the values and preconceptions that define *the uniqueness that is a person.* The hope is that the surrogate acts in accord with the wishes and values of the patient. Sometimes that is very difficult.

Expose the Hidden Agenda

Every painful situation contains elements that can resist resolution. Rarely are these elements articulated when the decision needs to be made. If the participants can identity the feelings, hurts, goals that lie beneath the spoken word, good decisions are more likely to occur.

Mom, in her own home, is healthy. She insists she has a good support system of neighbors and friends. She has fallen a couple of times and does not feel safe in her house. Because she does not want to worry her family, she doesn't want to say this out loud. Her out-of-town daughter feels guilty that she is not there to help, but it is hard for her to express that thought. Instead she says, "Mom, I just want you to be happy. Let's look at nursing homes." Mom protests. The truth is unspoken. The conversation is deadlocked. Here both parties have hidden agenda. Mom doesn't want to worry her daughter and she fears being forced from her home; daughter has guilt that she is not carrying properly for her mother.

Decision-makers revisit many a shoulda, woulda, coulda—often when it is too late. Guilt often comes into bloom at the funeral home in an expensive spray of roses. "Maybe these flowers will make me feel better about my neglect of Mom." They won't. At the time of decision-making, it is important to name and deal with as much of the underlying emotional reality as possible.

Decide What Is Good

It is never easy to make decisions concerning illness, aging, and death. The best result will be what a good friend once dubbed "one's reasonable best." We must make decisions in an instance of time with only the relevant facts *available at the time* and under the emotional conditions or urgency of the choice. Decisions are never perfect. If I had the time to think about the dilemma more thoroughly, if I hadn't been up all night waiting for the test results, if I were not so upset, if I didn't live a continent away from Dad . . . That is all true.

In real life, though, if-filled stories have imperfect endings. Human beings, flawed, can do only the possible. A thorough thoughtful process can help that happen. Decisions can never be best, but they *can* always be good.

Appendix B

Questions for Discussion

FOR INDIVIDUALS OR GROUPS who wish to go beyond reading these stories for their own sake, the questions below provide focus for discussion. They are grouped by the essay titles. There is some comparative overlap. The instructor or discussion leader can select those questions that are most helpful for their group, as not all questions are pertinent to every situation.

Note that some questions are appropriate for undergraduate students or lay discussion groups. Some are specific to professional groups. These require some degree of medical or ethical background. Appendix A will help.

Illness

Impotence

1. What did you feel as you read this story? Did you identify with any of the characters? What would you do if this patient were you? Defend your answer with moral reasoning.

2. Do you agree with the conclusion that turning off the machine and allowing natural death is moral? Give a basis for your answer.

3. Who should decide? Since the patient cannot *act* for himself, should someone else be forced to comply with his decision? What if the patient's wife, doctor, or other care givers believe turning off the machine is an immoral decision (suicide)? Does the patient's wish trump their beliefs? (Autonomy affords person a right to *pursue* suicide—a negative right. It does not guarantee that person help in doing so,

particularly if it compromises others' conscience or the law. Do you disagree? On what basis?)

4. What is the moral jurisdiction or obligation of those other than the patient to urge (read: arm twist) the patient to make a different decision?

5. Is cost of care a reason to stop treatment in this case? Why or why not?

6. Make a moral argument for the opposite position you took earlier.

7. Does the hospital have a moral stake here?

Row 30

1. What should a person with a serious illness consider in making treatment decisions?

2. Are cost, age, or family situation pertinent to such discussions? Why or why not?

3. What are the obligations of the professional "advisor" (doctor, nurse practitioner, etc.) to facilitate informed consent?

4. Would it have been a morally right decision for this anonymous woman to refuse treatment? Give reasons for your answer.

5. Cost dictated how and where she could be helped. Do people have an inherent positive right to accessible treatment, regardless of cost? Should payment be the obligation of the government? If so, what might be the scope of such obligation (minimal treatment, optional treatment such as elective surgery for obesity, cosmetic purposes, sterilization, gender change, for example)?

6. What obligation, if any, does the ordinary citizen have to the well-being and health of others?

7. Do you agree with the message of the quote at the beginning of the piece? Explain.

APPENDIX B

Red Sprinkles

1. Thin body image is the model that preoccupies many young girls. What cultural messages feed into this? Who, if anyone, has the responsibility to address this cultural problem?

2. Were Mary Claire's actions morally culpable? Why or why not?

3. Respond to Mary Claire's thesis that God would be pleased with her "fasting."

4. Have you known anyone with this problem? Does that influence how you might decide? How so?

A Trip to the Cabbage Patch

1. Considering the cost of bypass surgery and her age (mid-seventies), should the patient in this case say no to surgery? What relevant facts should be considered?

2. Would your answer change if she were younger and/or did not have medical insurance?

3. Let's assume the patient told the doctor that, after surgery, she would continue to eat poorly, refuse to take any medications, and not maintain a healthy lifestyle. If you were the surgeon, would you refuse to do the surgery? Give a moral basis for your answer.

4. Did the long-term psychic dimensions surprise you? As a professional, how should you deal with this aspect?

Hard Choices in the Garden of Good and Evil

1. Describe the pain Janet and her family experience as they deal with both her dad's and her illness. Does the same challenge over so many years alter how Bill's decision should be made?

2. At one point in the story Janet talks about her thoughts about pills for dementia. Name some of the commercials for medication you have seen on television. Choose one and analyze what it suggests will occur if the medication is chosen. What side effects does it have? Do you

believe the pros and cons featured in the ads are discussed in a balanced manner?

3. What should Bill consider as he struggles with his decision about his relationship with Elaine? Does or should his passion for justice or religious beliefs contribute anything to his consideration?

4. If Bill were to make that choice, would extra-marital sex in this situation differ morally from that in a case where the two married parties are competent and aware? Why or why not? Does the moral decision you think is the best one in this case differ from that in *Sex in Green Garden* (in next section)? What moral elements affect your answer?

5. Do you think Bill should break up with Elaine, divorce Janet and marry Elaine, or simply remain in the situation described? Give both moral and practical reasons for your response. What moral principles or method is at work in your decision?

6. Should Bill seek others' advice before he makes a final decision? Why or why not?

Please!

1. List the values that were important to Mom. How did she rank them?

2. There are several moral actors in this scenario: Susan, Susan's mother, the hospice institution, the individual care givers. Name the precise moral dilemma that each must face. (Hint: legal and cost issues may color decisions for each stakeholder.)

3. Put yourself in each of the roles above. What would you say?

4. Given the medical condition that Mom is in, who is the person/group that makes the final decision? On what basis?

5. Would it be morally appropriate for the hospice staff to carry out Susan's decision? Why or why not?

6. What were the conflicting values that Susan exhibited? Was she trying to hasten her mother's death? Describe the emotional overlay that colored her decision-making (see section 5 in Appendix 1). If you were a member of the ethics committee, what would you ask or add to the discussion?

7. What criteria, if any, justify usurping the autonomy and/or clear wishes of patients no longer able to speak for themselves?

Aging

Let's Be Frank: Don't Get Old

1. There are really two characters in this story: Frank and the narrator. Discuss the influence Frank had on his daughter's beliefs on illness and death.

2. Discuss your own beliefs about illness and death. What stories or experiences helped form those beliefs? What implications do your personal beliefs have for serious medical decisions?

3. Was it better for Frank to die young, given how he felt?

4. Change the narrative. Frank has a serious stroke, which incapacitates him but does not kill. If you were the daughter (or his medical professional) and Frank asked for you to help him die, what would you do? Give a moral basis for the answer.

5. Answer the questions that the author poses at the end of the piece. What moral criteria, if any, differentiate the euthanizing of pets from that of human beings?

6. We call assisted dying "euthanasia." The Greek word means "good death." Some countries and some state laws allow either assisted suicide or euthanasia. Is this a good idea? Give substantive reasons for your answer.

Interview with Ivy

1. What feelings did you have listening to Ivy's story?

2. When should a parent lose the say as to how to spend the last years of his or her life? Should this change in the case of serious dementia? A serious fall? Some other crisis?

3. Is Ivy doing so well *because* she is aging in place? Because her spouse is still alive?

4. Would you have any advice for the interviewer? For Ivy?

5. List the things that seem to keep Ivy and Alan going.

6. Can Ivy's, or anyone's advance directives account for all circumstances?

It's Time

1. What was the moral justification for the institution's decision to force the professor to retire?

2. Are there ways to avoid or minimize the marginalization of the elderly in society? You may wish to divide into groups to brainstorm. Compare the professor's life with Ivy's.

3. What prompted the professor's final action?

4. Immanuel Kant believed that suicide destroys the very moral basis that affirms it: the right to autonomy. It goes against a fundamental human value, he believed. What do you think?

5. Are there circumstances where ending a human life is morally justifiable? Were those circumstances present here?

A Visit to Sunny Hill

1. Describe the conditions of this nursing home. Note both the good and the bad.

2. Have you ever visited or worked in a nursing home? How does your experience correspond to the description here?

3. What moral issues do you see for Manny himself, for the family, for nursing home staff? What are the particular areas where each has proper jurisdiction? How much autonomy should each have in his or her purview?

4. As a medical professional, on what criteria would you depend in recommending a home?

Appendix B

Sex in Green Garden

1. Contrast the description of facilities in Sunny Hill and Green Garden. If you had to decide to recommend one or the other, what would you consider?

2. Given the stories about nursing homes and the narrative about Ivy, compare the pros and cons of each aging trajectory.

3. Should Eve be told? Why or why not? Can the relationship between Elmer and Lilith be consenting, when the parties have diminished capacity?

4. Should the relationship be stopped? Are one's sexual choices in a nursing home different from outside? Does the home have any jurisdiction over this private matter?

5. Consider the meeting of the Green Garden staff with Eve. Give each participant a moral perspective: religious person who thinks all extramarital sex is sinful, a libertarian—anything goes, etc. Have a virtual meeting and discuss this situation. The purpose of the meeting is to decide what, if anything, should be done. While an ethics committee is generally consultative rather than decision-making, this issue may have impact on the mission or rules of the home.

House Call

1. What is your assessment of the doctor's actions?

2. Would it have been better to bring the patient into a hospital and do testing? Why or why not?

3. What is the difference in cost between home care and nursing home care? (If you do not know, do the research and report back to the group.)

4. Discuss the impact of taking an elderly woman to a hospital for observation.

5. Compare the aging situation of this woman with the people in the previous pieces. What are the pros and cons of each situation? Are there always choices?

Death

The Birthday Party

1. What emotions did you feel as you read this short piece?

2. Do you want to live as long as the woman in the story? Why or why not?

3. Describe the family dynamic. Should the care fall on a daughter-in-law, or should Emma have been sent to assisted living? What criteria contribute to your answer?

4. Who has the moral obligation to care for an elderly person? Should that person feel an obligation, like Bertha or an Inuit grandma who walks to her death on an ice floe to allow the tribe to move more quickly without her?

5. Should government assist in caring for fragile elderly at home? In a facility? Only if there is no one else to do so? Give reasons for your answer.

Last Rites

1. What duties, if any, do family members have regarding aging or dying parents?

2. Mary Ellen chose to cease treatment. Was this a morally right choice? Defend your answer.

3. Both this piece and *It's Time* as a whole detail the detachment of older folks from social and physical life. Do you believe this happens to the elderly? If so, what solutions might there be?

Bertha

1. Describe Bertha's personality. Notice how Bertha's internal story, her preconceptions, affect her choice.

2. If you were the daughter, which of the following would you have done? Give rationale for your answer.

   a) Support Bertha's decision

   b) Call in a psychiatrist and, if ordered, force Bertha to take meds for depression (evidence for depression?)

   c) Have a feeding tube placed

   d) Tell Bertha she was committing a sin

   e) Respect Bertha's autonomy, no matter how difficult this is

3. Was Bertha's act suicide? Why or why not? Does it differ from the decision to stop treatment (previous narrative)?

4. Differentiate between the terms *active* and *passive* in this case.

5. If you were Bertha, what would you have done? What personal stories do you have that affect this decision?

6. Contrast this story with the one you read about Manny ("A Visit to Sunny Hill").

7. Should Bertha's family have tried to treat her more aggressively? Would your answer change if she were younger or if she had no medical insurance? Give reasons for your answer.

8. Do Bertha or Manny or any of the persons described in these stories have a different idea about what quality of life or health is? Describe. What is health to you?

This Is My Body

1. What criteria should be used before deciding to perform resuscitation?

2. Does this case fit those guidelines?

3. If you do not know, find out how often a resuscitated person goes back to baseline function after the procedure.

4. Knowing those statistics, what would you advise another about including a DNR (do not resuscitate) order in an advance directive? Do you have that in your own DNR?

5. In your personal or professional experience, do you believe death always brings people together? Why or why not?

Saying Goodbye

1. Have you a bucket list? If you are a professional or training to be one, should you ever suggest this kind of thing to patients? Why or why not?

2. Are some topics too personal?

3. Note that the story doesn't have any indication that the narrator works or volunteers or has any occupation other than musing on her life. Sounds as if the narrator is a pretty "privileged" person. What do you think?

4. What moral obligations does an older person have to self, family, the greater community?